CW00664350

Peter Leach lives and works in Somerset as an archaeological consultant, and has been involved in the archaeology of the county for over 30 years. Since graduating from the University of Wales, Cardiff, he has been a field officer with the Committee for Rescue Archaeology in Avon, Gloucestershire and Somerset, the Western Archaeological Trust in Bristol, and more recently a director of the Field Archaeology Unit at the University of Birmingham. In addition to his interests and work in Somerset he has also been involved in major research projects at Wharram Percy in Yorkshire, Sutton Hoo in Suffolk, and in Croatia as a member of the international Adriatic Islands Project research team. He is also a co-director of the South Cadbury Environs Research Project, under the aegis of the University of Bristol. He has published numerous papers and excavation reports, and is a Member of the Institute of Field Archaeologists and a Fellow of the Society of Antiquaries.

Following page
The gilded bronze head of Minerva, probably from the main cult statue located within the temple of Sulis Minerva, Bath (*see page 38*).

ROMAN SOMERSET

Peter Leach

THE DOVECOTE PRESS

For Amma Dee

Hunting scene, fragment of a mosaic pavement from East Coker Roman villa.

First published in 2001 by The Dovecote Press Ltd
Stanbridge, Wimborne, Dorset BH21 4JD

ISBN 1 874336 93 8

© Peter Leach 2001

Designed and produced by The Dovecote Press Ltd
Printed and bound by the Baskerville Press, Salisbury

Peter Leach has asserted his right under the Copyright Designs and
Patent Act 1988 to be identified as author of this work

A CIP catalogue record of this book is
available from the British Library

All rights reserved

1 3 5 7 9 8 6 4 2

Contents

Introduction & Acknowledgements

This is the first book devoted to the Roman period in Somerset, a place which did not exist until early medieval times. For the 350 years Somerset was part of the Roman empire it was split three ways into administrative units that were based upon long-standing pre-Roman tribal divisions and identities. To an extent these divisions persist to this day, perpetuated by the political creations of North Somerset, and Bath and North East Somerset; while the contrasts between Exmoor and the west, and the rest of the county could hardly be greater. These contrasts are of course what give the county its unique character and appeal today, and it is only right that this survey should cover the entire historic county of Somerset.

In the century since Francis Haverfield gave the first account of Roman Somerset, in the now long out of date volume I of the *Victoria County History of Somerset*, our knowledge and understanding of the dynamics of Roman Britain have been transformed. Almost all of our information for the Roman period is based upon archaeological evidence, and in the past three decades or so there has been a huge increase in this data from Somerset (in common with many other parts of Britain), arising from excavations, field survey and chance discoveries.

A great deal of this information has resulted from development – road building, quarrying, building works, etc. – and the evolution of archaeological responses to it, which attempt to control its impact and ensure that remains can be protected or recorded wherever possible. Somerset's museums and the Sites and Monuments databases maintained by its local government authorities act as repositories for the discoveries and the basic information gathered, but its analysis and publication is of equal importance. Somerset is fortunate in the range and quality of archaeological publications which have been produced, particularly in recent years, although much still remains unpublished as the current volume of discoveries continues undiminished.

This account is thus inevitably a snapshot, and to some extent a personal account, of a time and a place as we conceive it, taken at the beginning of the twenty-first century. In a publication of this size it has been impossible to cover more than a selection of sites – another book could certainly be written to include an almost completely different set

– in itself an indication of just how rich and diverse the evidence for Roman Somerset now is! While its errors and omissions must for the most part be my responsibility, I am grateful to numerous friends and colleagues for assistance or encouragement in bringing it to fruition. My thanks in particular to Peter Ellis and to David Burnett at Dovecote Press, for their considerable editorial input and support; to Bob Croft and other members of the Archaeology Section in Somerset County Council, to Steve Minnitt and staff at the County Museum in Taunton, to Richard Tabor and to Charles and Nancy Hollinrake. And finally I owe a special debt of gratitude to Philip Rahtz, who introduced me to Somerset's archaeology more than thirty years ago and who has inspired me ever since.

Acknowledgement and thanks are due to all those who provided illustrations: The Bath Archaeological Trust for the illustrations on pages 35, 45 and 51; Birmingham University Field Archaeology Unit for pages 68, 77 and 115; Archaeology Section, Bristol City Museum for page 121; Collingwood, R. G. and Wright R. P. *The Roman Inscriptions of Britain,* 1965, (1672 and 1673) for page 55; Devon County Council for page 92; Jim Easthaugh for page 13; Kevin Green, *The Archaeology of the Roman Economy*, 1986, (fig. 36) for page 118; Nancy Hollinrake for the maps on pages 8 and 28; North Somerset Museum Service for page 102; The Roman Baths Museum for the frontispiece, the back cover, and pages 39, 40, 41, 43, 44, 49, 107 and 113; Somerset Archaeology and Natural History Society for pages 4, 82 and 88; Somerset County Council for pages 18, 21, 29, 70, 74, 78, 101; Somerset County Museum for the front cover and pages 16, 20, 24, 25, 71, 75, 85, 93, 98, 99, 100 and 104; Wells Museum for page 22; Yeovil Archaeological and Local History Society for page 87.

PETER LEACH
Pilton, Somerset
OCTOBER 2001

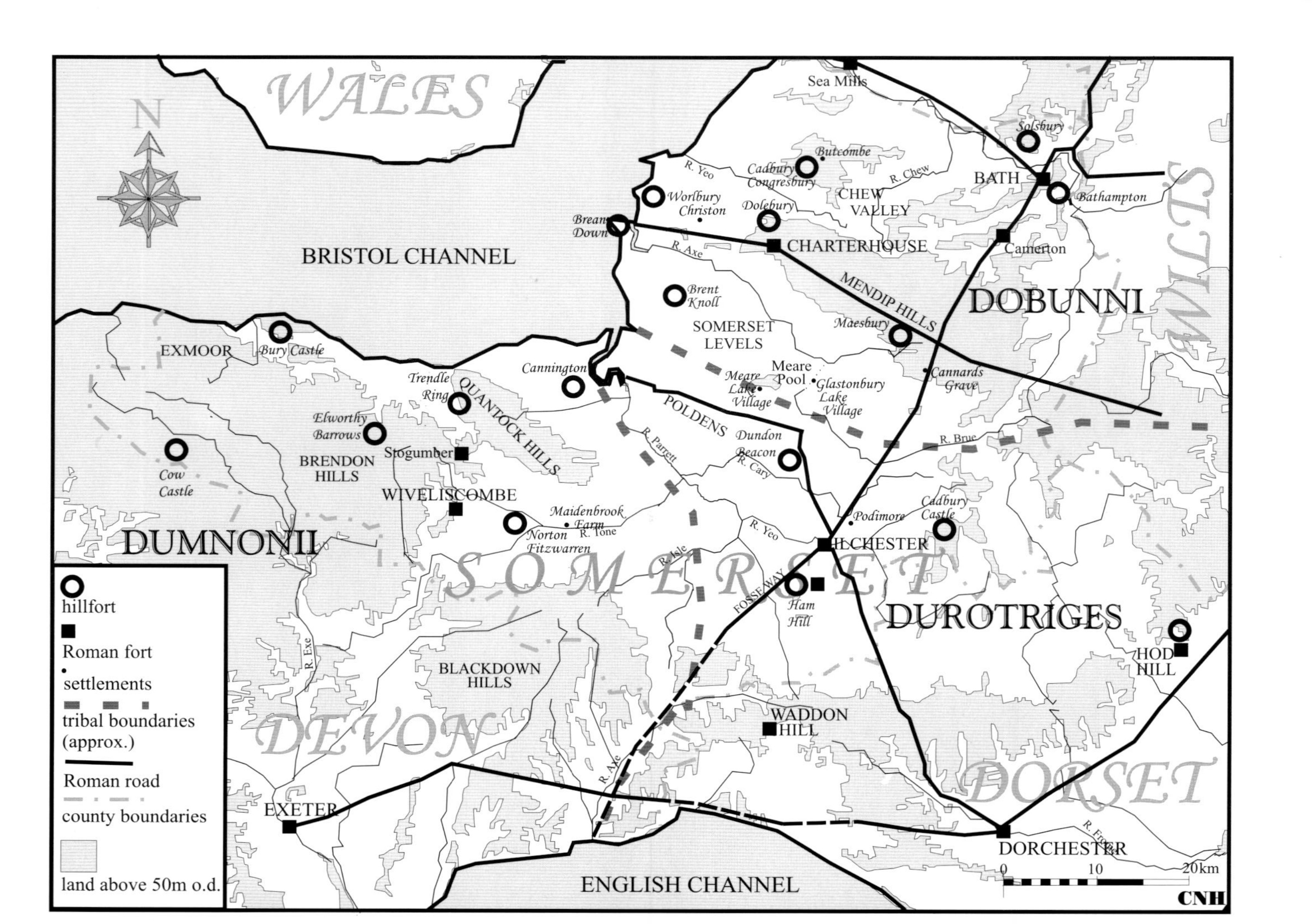

WALES
WILTS
SOMERSET
DEVON
DORSET
BRISTOL CHANNEL
ENGLISH CHANNEL
DOBUNNI
DUROTRIGES
DUMNONII
Sea Mills
Solsbury
BATH
Bathampton
Camerton
Cadbury Congresbury
Butcombe
CHEW VALLEY
R. Chew
CHARTERHOUSE
Dolebury
Worlebury
Christon
R. Yeo
R. Axe
Brean Down
Brent Knoll
MENDIP HILLS
Maesbury
Cannards Grave
SOMERSET LEVELS
Meare Lake Village
Meare Pool
Glastonbury Lake Village
POLDENS
Dundon Beacon
R. Cary
R. Brue
Cadbury Castle
Podimore
ILCHESTER
Ham Hill
FOSSEWAY
R. Yeo
R. Parrett
R. Isle
Cannington
QUANTOCK HILLS
Trendle Ring
Stogumber
Maidenbrook Farm
R. Tone
Norton Fitzwarren
WIVELISCOMBE
Elworthy Barrows
BRENDON HILLS
Bury Castle
EXMOOR
Cow Castle
BLACKDOWN HILLS
WADDON HILL
HOD HILL
R. Frome
DORCHESTER
R. Axe
R. Exe
EXETER
N
0
10
20km
CNH
hillfort
Roman fort
settlements
tribal boundaries (approx.)
Roman road
county boundaries
land above 50m o.d.

ONE

Somerset before Rome

When the future emperor of Rome, Vespasian, led his troops into Somerset in either AD 43 or 44, no such place existed, either politically or geographically. Modern Somerset was an Anglo-Saxon creation, the ultimate successor to Roman administration and its aftermath in this region of Britain. At the time of the Roman Conquest of Britain what is now Somerset was divided between the territories of three major native tribes, identified by the Romans as the Dobunni, the Durotriges and the Dumnonii.

The Dobunni controlled north Somerset, roughly from the southern flanks of the Mendip Hills northwards; their territories extending north up the Severn Valley and including most of the Cotswolds. South Somerset and the Levels were Durotrigan territory, whose lands also encompassed most of present day Dorset and south-west Wiltshire. To the west were the Dumnonii, occupying the south-west peninsula of Devon and Cornwall, with an eastern boundary in Somerset that was probably the River Parrett. These were indigenous political entities recognised by Rome, and peopled by the native Iron Age inhabitants of the region: but who were these tribespeople and how were they affected by this devastating foreign invasion?

PREHISTORY

Man probably made his earliest appearance in Somerset some half a million years ago, as a transient hunter and gatherer of food, in a landscape and environment very different from that of today. Towards the end of the last Ice Age, some 12,000 – 13,000 years ago, our modern ancestors were occupying caves at Cheddar and Wookey on the Mendip Hills. From about 4000 BC Somerset was being transformed by the impact of agriculture, but it was not until well into the Bronze Age – around 1500 BC - that Somerset's peoples (as elsewhere in Britain) adopted a more settled way of life. A growing population was expanding into new areas; a process reflected both in the reorganisation of society and by its impact on the environment. Identified settlement

Opposite page. A general map showing the geography and principal sites in Somerset at the time of the Roman Conquest in AD 43 or 44.

sites are still a rarity, but hilltops such as Norton Fitzwarren, near Taunton, and both Ham Hill and Cadbury Castle gained a new importance as Somerset saw a massive expansion in agricultural production and land clearance from about 1,000 BC onwards.

THE IRON AGE

The period we call the Iron Age in Britain began during the eighth century BC. In reality, the changes occurring several centuries earlier towards the end of the Bronze Age are just as crucial. During the millennium prior to the coming of Rome, both the political and economic landscape of Somerset was transformed. A growing population, combined with the expansion and intensification of agriculture, put a greater emphasis upon land ownership, and saw the evolution of a more hierarchical tribal system. Inevitably, communities identified themselves more intimately with particular landscapes and territories, and the influence of chieftains and religious leaders like the Druids increased. All of this probably intensified rivalry between groups and individuals, although the larger ethnic tribal groups recognised by the incoming Roman government probably originated then, if not in earlier times.

What Rome certainly inherited at the time of the Conquest was a populous and settled landscape of productive fields, meadows, broad upland pastures, woodland and fen. The great bulk of Somerset's Iron Age peoples lived by agriculture, inhabiting hamlets and individual farms throughout the county. Chance discoveries show that many coincide approximately with the location of both Roman and medieval successors, and it was surely in this time that much of the framework of our modern countryside was created. Aerial photography and field surveys are now revealing just how widespread these settlements were, and something of their character, although the most detailed information comes from excavated sites.

What must surely be the most famous Iron Age village in Britain was excavated at Glastonbury in the late nineteenth and early twentieth centuries. This, and the neighbouring village at Meare, were exceptionally well preserved in the waterlogged conditions on the edge of a former lake, and provide a vivid picture of daily life in a Somerset community towards the end of the Iron Age. Given their location, these settlements may not be wholly typical of the majority in the county. It has been suggested that because they lay close to the boundary between the three major tribal groups, they also acted as a meeting place for both social and material exchanges between communities.

Elsewhere in Somerset, other excavations have explored more selective samples of native settlements, though nowhere has yet equalled the wealth of preservation seen in the Lake Villages. In the west,

Reconstruction of a typical Iron Age house at the Glastonbury Lake Village, Peat Moors Visitor Centre, Westhay.

settlements were typically enclosed by a bank and ditch, and are likely to have been individual farmsteads housing no more than extended families. Such sites are also common further east, but with less emphasis on defensive enclosures, as at Maidenbrook Farm near Taunton, Cannards Grave, Shepton Mallet, Camerton, or Butcombe. At Heriots Bridge in the Chew Valley, Christon (destroyed by the M5) and Podimore near Ilchester were larger, village-like settlements, and many more of these undoubtedly remain to be discovered. Apart from Christon, all of these sites were succeeded by Roman settlements.

Perhaps the most visible monuments to the activity of the Iron Age peoples of this region are its hillforts. Somerset is well endowed with such sites; there are 50 or so major examples, and at least as many smaller enclosures, ranging in size from the massive 85 hectares of Ham Hill to small sites of less than 1 hectare (e.g. Bury Castle, Cow Castle, or Trendle Ring on the Quantock Hills). They occur widely across the county, from Exmoor in the west to Bath in the east, although their distribution is by no means even. Some of the largest and most impressive, with multiple ramparts and strongly defended entrances, are in the south and east of the county. Examples include Ham Hill, Cadbury Castle, Solsbury, Dolebury and Brent Knoll. West of the River Parrett smaller enclosures are more common.

Excavated foundations of a circular Iron Age house, Cannards Grave, Shepton Mallet.

Despite their numbers, few hillforts have been much excavated. Thus, little is known of their individual histories, and even their function is still unclear. In Somerset, only Cadbury Castle has been extensively excavated to modern standards, making it one of the templates for Iron Age society in southern Britain. Cadbury Castle appears to have been intensively occupied over many centuries, right up to the Roman Conquest, and was effectively the 'capital' of one of the most powerful tribes in this part of Somerset. At times it was perhaps the residence of a chief, at others a place of refuge or defence. But it was also a social, ritual and religious centre; a place which somehow personified its people, their particular identity, and that of their region.

Not all hillforts were intensively occupied. Some appear to have had fairly limited or intermittent periods of use; while others, particularly those in the western half of the county, were too small to house a large community, or were too exposed to be suitable for long-term residence. Indeed, many of the west Somerset sites are more akin to the pattern of small defended settlements which typify both the Iron Age and Roman periods in Wales and the South West.

Hillforts have been compared to medieval castles; strongholds occupied by chieftains and their retainers, dominating and protecting groups of undefended settlements within their tribal territories, who periodically went to war with their neighbours and rivals. While there may be some truth in this, it is far from being the whole story. In many instances their function, and even their physical form and location, is as

Cadbury Castle from the south, South Cadbury.

likely to have been symbolic; representing the status and identity of a tribal community, its rituals, and its ancestral claims to land and territory in a harsh and often fiercely competitive environment. Thus Ham Hill and Cadbury Castle for example, may have been the focus of neighbouring tribal territories in south Somerset, originally perhaps rivals, but eventually to be allies in the face of Rome.

SIGNS AND PORTENTS

The Romans first came to Britain in 55 BC, and again the following year, under the command of Julius Caesar. Both expeditions were really just an extension of Caesar's Gallic campaigns, which absorbed Gaul (France) into the Empire. Caesar's British adventure fell victim to military and political pressures on the Continent, forcing his eventual withdrawal to Rome. Thus, Rome's conquest of Britain was delayed for almost a century, but even this brief contact had a significant impact upon the native British.

Until the second century BC Britain lay very much on the periphery of the known world. Direct contact between the Mediterranean and this remote northern island was rare and sporadic. Even Caesar found it necessary to mount a ship-borne reconnaissance to gain more intelligence. Despite this relative lack of knowledge, Rome's influence had already crossed the Channel, a process that probably began with the annexation of the Mediterranean coastal region of Gaul, centred on Marseilles. One effect of this was to stimulate trade and exchange with

Floods in the Yeo Valley reveal the circular Iron Age *oppidum* enclosure (centre top) at Ilchester (top left); and the line of the Fosse Way (centre).

the Celtic tribes in the rest of Gaul, and ultimately with their British cousins. There may already have been fairly close cultural links between Britain and Gaul, which were now stimulated by the demands of the enormous new and voracious market to the south. There was also a political dimension to this influence, which may have brought some Belgic immigrants into parts of southern England, and perhaps some Gaulish control or influence over tribal affairs.

It has been suggested that the three-way split in tribal affiliations, which was so apparent at the time of the Roman conquest of Somerset, originated much earlier in the first millennium BC, if not before. Indirectly, Rome's influence certainly sharpened their definition. It was the Durotriges who were first to experience the effects, and in particular through their Armorican contacts. Regular contact between Armorica (roughly Brittany) and south-west Britain goes back at least to the fourth millennium BC, but its reinforcement through trade and the exchange of ideas and knowledge with the classical world from the second century BC, brought the two regions closer together. One effect was the founding of a trading port on the south coast, at Hengistbury Head in Dorset. Another was the appearance of coinage.

The Durotriges seem to have prospered for a while, exchanging both raw materials and finished products – iron, bronze, precious metals, metalwork, salt, hides, wool or cloth, livestock, agricultural produce, and probably slaves. Both imported and local gold and silver coins began to circulate within the Durotrigan realm, their distribution, along with that of a new and distinctive black burnished style of pottery, giving useful clues as to the extent of its territory.

The social and political impact of this period of contact is more difficult to assess, but may have exacerbated tensions already present within late Iron Age society. Hillforts like Cadbury and Ham Hill had their defences strengthened, as were the alliances between the northern Durotriges of Somerset and their Dorset cousins to the south. One structure that may have its origins at this time was a large embanked enclosure in the valley of the River Yeo, just south of Ilchester. Discovered only quite recently as a result of flooding, it comprised a broad bank and ditch enclosing an oval area of at least 16 hectares. Little excavation has taken place, although there is evidence of some occupation at two places inside the bank, and the remains of a low stone revetment on its outer face. This site appears to represent some new form of centre within the region, perhaps analogous to the much larger enclosures known as *oppida*, that were then appearing in south-eastern England and in Gaul. They seem to have developed as tribal centres of political, economic and religious importance; the first stage in the emergence of towns. The site at Ilchester may not have aspired to quite that status, its valley-bottom location making it anyway unsuitable for more than seasonal occupation. However, it does seem to reflect the changing times; the need for a new centre and focus for trade and exchange, for some social and political transactions; located, perhaps, on neutral ground away from, though still within the orbit of major hillfort-centred territories.

Excavation of the stone revetment fronting the *oppidum* rampart remains at Ilchester.

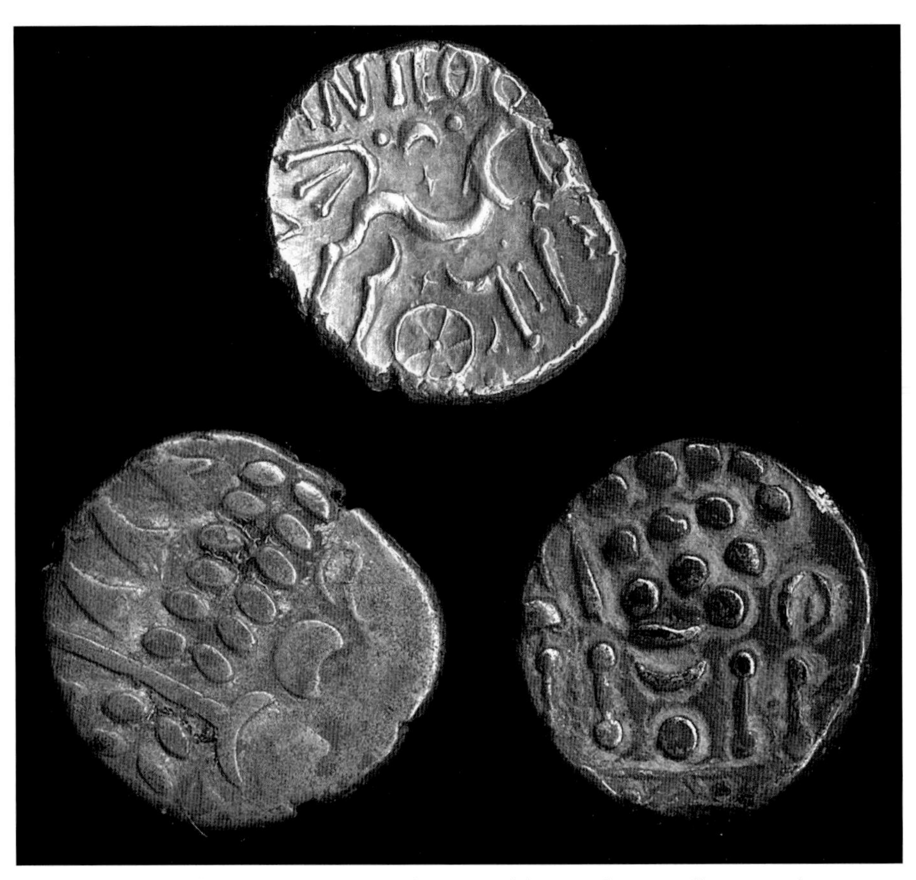

Iron Age coins from Somerset. A Dobunnic gold stater from Cadbury Castle (top); and Durotrigan silver coins from Ham Hill (bottom left) and South Petherton (bottom right).

The Dumnonii, whose territory bordered that of the Durotriges in west Somerset, also shared in this phase of strengthened contacts with Armorica, although it is likely that these two regions had shared close links over a much longer period. No coinage was adopted in the region, and it is difficult to perceive any obvious political or social changes at this time, particularly in west Somerset.

North Somerset lay within the sphere of the Dobunni, whose heartland's lay in what is now Gloucestershire. An indigenous coinage was not in circulation there until after Caesar's expeditions, but its distribution in north Somerset, along with another style of pottery, suggests that historically this region had a distinct cultural and political identity. North Somerset also has a high density of major hillforts, some of which were almost certainly refortified in this period. Evidence of a massacre at Worlebury hillfort, near Weston-super-Mare, may be another reflection of stress and conflicts within society at this time, although reliable evidence from excavation on such sites is sparse. A concentration of late Iron Age coins, metalwork and pottery in the Camerton area hint at the possibility of a new regional centre there, while the nearby hot springs at Bath were undoubtedly an important focus well before their Roman development.

Almost a century separates the expeditions of Julius Caesar from the invasion of the Emperor Claudius. Caesar's accounts of his expeditions give us valuable insights into the way of life of the indigenous Britons during their final years of independence. There are glimpses of their wealth and relative prosperity, formidable abilities in warfare, religious practices and the power of the Druids, and their tribal organisation under separate kings or high chiefs – frequently at odds with each other but capable of combining to face a common threat.

The defeat of the Armorican tribes by Caesar and their incorporation into the new Roman province of Gaul, disrupted and then apparently brought to a halt the cross-Channel exchange and alliances which had flourished for over half a century. The focus of prosperity shifted to south-eastern England, whose tribes were now in close contact with Gaul and the Empire; exporting raw materials and products in exchange for luxury items such as metalwork, fine pottery, glass and wine. The minting and use of gold and silver coinage became more widespread, and with the development of *oppida* the movement towards a more centralised political system and the consolidation of tribal identities intensified. This period may mark the appearance of suspected tribal centres at Ilchester and perhaps also at Camerton. Both gold and silver coinage was now being minted and used in Dobunnic north Somerset, but the Durotriges were evidently suffering by their former alliances with Armorica and the disruption of trade, since their coinage became progressively debased to predominantly silver and finally to just bronze issues before the end of the first century BC.

TWO

Conquest & Consolidation

THE CLAUDIAN CONQUEST

In the century following Caesar's expeditions Britain remained on the minds of Rome and her rulers. To some extent it was even a thorn in their side as they attempted to pacify the newly conquered province of Gaul. At the same time, however, some British tribes and their leaders were forging stronger links and perhaps even alliances with their new imperial neighbour. At least two emperors, Augustus and Caligula, made plans for invasion, but it was their heir Claudius who finally turned plans into reality, landing four legions of about 45,000 troops at Richborough in Kent in July of AD 43. Claudius rapidly subjugated the tribes of south-eastern England, by a combination of fiercely fought battles and peace treaties with more friendly tribes. Despite these early successes, this was only the beginning of a forty-year long campaign to bring the rest of Britain within the Empire.

One of the legions brought to Britain by Claudius, the Legio II Augusta, was commanded by Vespasian, whose task it was to secure and

The Iron Age hillfort, Ham Hill. An aerial view from the north which also shows the extensive stone quarry workings.

Members of the 'Ermine Street Guard' dressed as Roman legionaries.

consolidate the south-west. Unlike Julius Caesar's Gallic Wars, we have no surviving contemporary account of Claudius's British conquest, although the Roman writer Suetonius summarised the campaign half a century later and further details have been gleaned from the works of later writers, notably Tacitus. There is no direct reference to the Durotriges or any of the other tribes occupying Somerset, but beginning with his capture of the Isle of Wight, Vespasian is credited with the conquest of more than twenty hillforts and the surrender of two powerful tribes. One of these was almost certainly the Durotriges, although the identity of the other is less clear. One possibility is the Dobunni of north Somerset, who may have split from their northern cousins; the latter evidently making their peace with Claudius soon after the invasion. Another is the Dumnonii to the south-west, within whose territory the legion was subsequently based for several years at Exeter.

Durotrigan hostility to Rome had a history extending back to the suppression of their Armorican allies by Julius Caesar. Reference to the capture of more than 20 *oppida* suggests that the Durotriges fell back upon their hillforts to resist the Roman advance, rather than risk pitched battles, as some of the tribes to the east had done. This strategy may also reflect a less cohesive and centralised tribal authority. Despite their apparent defensive strengths, the hillforts were no match for a professional army under the command of such a determined and implacable general as Vespasian. One by one they fell, and occasionally archaeology gives us a glimpse of the violence of that process.

In Somerset, possible evidence for localised armed resistance to the

Evidence of the Roman occupation of Ham Hill includes Roman armour, dress fittings and spearheads.

Roman advance can be traced to the remains of the massacred defenders found at the south-west gate of Cadbury Castle. A similar fate probably befell Ham Hill, where human burials have also been excavated among its defences. There is greater uncertainty regarding the fate of the north Somerset hillforts in Dobunnic territory, although it is unlikely that their continued occupation would have been tolerated, even if their people had submitted peacefully to Rome like their northern cousins. We are similarly ignorant of circumstances in the South West, although there is little evidence for military campaigning there, and the Dumnonii are more likely to have made their peace with Rome to forestall such an invasion.

MILITARY OCCUPATION

By AD 47 the first phase of the conquest was complete. The richest, south-eastern parts of Britain had been incorporated into the new province, and a military zone established within the territories of tribes to the north and west. Somerset lay firmly within this militarised zone; its inhabitants no doubt still smarting from their defeat at the hands of Vespasian's army, and suffering all the hardships of a conquered people.

To maintain her authority and keep the peace it was necessary for Rome to garrison her newly conquered territory, particularly in areas like Dorset and Somerset, where resistance had been fiercest. This was

The rectangular outlines of the Roman fort overlooking lead mining remains in the Velvet Bottom valley, Charterhouse on Mendip.

achieved by building forts to house garrisons, and roads to aid communications and the rapid movement of troops. Unlike parts of Britain further to the north and west, where the army stayed longer, we have little information of the disposition or identity of the units that garrisoned Somerset. The Legio II Augusta, initially under Vespasian, remained in the South West, although units of auxiliary troops recruited from other provinces in the Empire took responsibility for garrisoning many forts, as well as other duties. The principal base for the conquest of the Durotriges was at Lake Farm, near Wimborne; within easy reach of a supply base at Hamworthy on Poole Harbour, and where part of the legion was probably stationed.

Elsewhere, it was necessary to establish a series of forts at strategic locations to enforce Roman rule. In Somerset a fort appears to have been built within the Iron Age ramparts of Ham Hill, although now largely quarried away. At Ilchester, another fort was probably located close to an important river crossing, although its remains have yet to be verified. This is also the case at Bath, at another important river crossing. The best surviving fort remains in Somerset are at Charterhouse on the Mendip Hills, where early control over lead mining and the extraction

Lead pigs found at Green Ore, Mendip, produced during the reign of the emperor Vespasian, AD 69-79.

of silver was the principal objective. Lead and silver were being produced and exported from here by at least AD 49; leaving Britain as stamped lead pigs via Southampton. A road runs eastwards from the mines along the top of Mendip to Southampton, crossing Wiltshire via Salisbury.

The army played a major role in the layout and construction of Britain's road system in the years following the Conquest. One of the most important was the Fosse Way, which began originally near Bridport, Dorset, crossing Somerset via Ilchester, Shepton Mallet, and Bath. Another road linked Ilchester with Dorchester (probably the site of another fort), and ultimately with Poole Harbour. All of these routes played a vital role in supplying the army garrisons and for moving troops, and were built in the first decade of the Roman occupation.

The need to establish and man a series of forts within Durotrigan territory reflects not only their initial hostility to Rome, but perhaps also a relatively uncentralised tribal society. At the Conquest the Durotriges were probably still a loose confederation of sub-chiefdoms. The troops garrisoning the region had to be located close to (and in some cases inside) the main local centres of power within the tribal territories. Forts at both Ilchester and within Ham Hill suggest that area to be the main seat of Durotrigan power within Somerset, and probably the most densely settled. No other forts of the Conquest period have yet been recognised in their territory, although other potential sites within Dobunnic territory include Camerton and Shepton Mallet.

Historical sources tell us that the conquest and consolidation of Britain was a protracted affair, as its Roman rulers attempted to assert authority over the island by a combination of treaties with friendly tribes, and military conquest where diplomacy failed. Within a few years of Claudius's conquest, Britain's governors were forced to intervene militarily in Wales, a region that was not finally subjugated until Agricola's campaign of AD 78. A diplomatic solution may originally have obviated the need for military action in the South West, but by the early 50s this policy was perhaps no longer tenable.

A new legionary fortress was established for Legio II Augusta at Exeter by about AD 55, and several forts were built within Dumnonian territory at around this time. The most easterly of these was at Wiveliscombe, where some earthworks survive. This fort was probably built to oversee both the uplands of the Quantock and Brendon Hills, as well as the more populous Vale of Taunton Deane. Recent aerial reconnaissance has also identified a possible signal station near Stogumber, which could be of the same period. Like the earlier forts within Durotrigan territory, those in the South West were required to garrison an essentially fragmented tribal society, living in small scattered settlements, and where little or no movement towards centralisation of power had occurred prior to the Conquest. Such societies were always more difficult to regulate and police within the Roman imperial system, and help explain why the most Romanised parts of Britain were always the south and east.

Whatever the circumstances in the South West at this time, the Roman administration was soon faced with a serious threat to its tenure. Amongst the tribes that rapidly made a treaty with Rome in the wake of the Conquest was the Iceni of East Anglia. Along with the Regni of Sussex, the Iceni were allowed to retain a degree of independence and autonomy within the new province, under their king, Prasutagus. However, his death in AD 59 prompted moves to integrate the Iceni more fully into the province, a process whose heavy-handedness outraged both the aristocracy and the royal family. The outcome was a revolt led by the king's widow, Boudicca (Bodicea), which rapidly gained popular support from other disaffected tribespeople in the South East, and led to the defeat of several army detachments and the sacking of newly founded towns at Colchester, St Albans and London. The initial success of the revolt was doubtless aided by the fact that most of the army of occupation was busy attempting to finally subdue resistance in North Wales. This campaign was rapidly aborted, and the then governor of Britain, Suetonius Paulinus, was forced to return and eventually defeat

Excavation of the south-west gate passage and defences of Cadbury Castle.

Boudicca and her forces in a pitched battle somewhere in the south-east of England in AD 60.

We have no certain evidence that the native peoples of Somerset took part in this revolt, but it is surely significant that according to the account of the writer Tacitus, the commander of the Second Legion at Exeter declined to move in support of the governor against the Boudiccan rebels on his return from North Wales. The commander's fate for this refusal was to take his own life, but it was surely the fear of a further major revolt by the Durotriges, if not some of their neighbours, which prompted his paying so high a price for his caution. Indeed, one piece of evidence which suggests that his fears were not unfounded, came from the excavations at Cadbury Castle.

One of the most dramatic discoveries during the Cadbury excavations were of human remains associated with the destruction by fire of the hillfort's latest Iron Age south-west gate. These remains, which included men, women and children, have been interpreted as the victims of a massacre that occurred as the gate was stormed and the hillfort captured by Roman troops. It is now clear that following the attack the remains of the victims in the passageway were sealed beneath a new entrance passage and defended gateway, which was itself destroyed again several years later. Following this action a detachment of troops was stationed briefly within the hillfort, occupying a timber barrack block near the summit of the hill.

We cannot pinpoint the precise date of these events, but the Boudiccan uprising provides the most likely context. Apart from the evidence of unrest in Somerset at this time, perhaps the most surprising realisation is that the hillfort continued in use throughout the period following its initial capture in AD 43 or 44. One further aspect of this re-use seems to have been the building of a wooden shrine (see chapter 8), perhaps to commemorate those who died. It is unlikely that this would have been tolerated without official Roman approval, and such early post-Conquest occupations must be considered as a possibility within some others of the county's hillforts.

One other hint of a military response to the instability of these times was the construction of a new fort at Ilchester. Beneath the later Roman town, excavations have revealed the outlines of a rectangular ditched enclosure covering approximately 7 hectares, with traces of an inner bank in places, and a double ditch separated by a palisade along its east side. Little of its interior arrangement is known, although the Fosse Way may mark the line of the main internal street. Alongside the Fosse Way,

Celtic bronze face plaque found in the remains of the south-west gate, Cadbury Castle.

immediately south of the fort, were contemporary timber-framed buildings representing either an associated depot area, or the beginnings of a civilian settlement. Outside the defences to the west were a series of gravel pits which had been backfilled with refuse from the fort. These remains are dated approximately to between the early 60s and mid 70s AD, the most likely period of military occupation.

A fort of this size, lying between the fairly standard smaller auxiliary forts and a bigger legionary fortress such as Exeter, might imply that part of the Second Legion was based here, although we have no direct evidence. The finds (coins, pottery, glass, metalwork, food remains, etc.), that suggest its period of occupation, do not, unfortunately, give precise enough information about its foundation date. Ilchester's fort could either have been a response to the Boudiccan troubles, or have been founded a few years earlier, perhaps when the legion moved its headquarters to Exeter.

The Boudiccan revolt caused considerable disruption to the progress towards civil government and development of the province in the South East. Its after effect in Somerset is more difficult to be sure of. The episode of resistance documented at Cadbury Castle may only have been a relatively isolated incident, and it looks as though Somerset's army garrisons were ultimately successful in pacifying the region and preparing the way for it to become part of an emerging civil province of Britain.

The Legio II Augusta spent little more than a decade at their Exeter base before being moved north to Gloucester in either AD 66 or 67. This was mainly in response to the renewal of campaigning in Wales, and suggests that the South West was largely peaceful by that date. Some of the forts in Somerset may have retained their garrisons for a few more years, particularly at places like Bath and Ilchester, with their strategic locations and communication links, but they had almost certainly been vacated by the early 70s. Even at the Charterhouse lead and silver mines on Mendip, private entrepreneurs appear to have been taking over production in the reign of the now emperor Vespasian (AD 69-79), which supports archaeological evidence that the fort there was no longer garrisoned.

THREE

Town & Country

Despite the turmoil and upheaval suffered by Somerset and its people during the middle years of the first century AD, within a generation or so the region was firmly established within the new province of Britannia. It was not until the victory of its governor Agricola over the Caledonian tribes of northern Scotland in AD 84 that the conquest was complete. Even then Rome's hold on Scotland was tenuous and eventually not sustained north of Hadrian's Wall. Few if any military detachments were left in Somerset, and governors like Agricola were actively fostering regional self-government.

THE FACE OF THE LAND

What was Somerset like when Vespasian marched in at the head of his legion and auxiliary troops to claim it for Rome? Within it borders, the county boasts one of the most diverse landscapes in Britain; from sea cliffs and high moorland, to lowland fens, fertile river valleys, limestone downland and clay vales. It owes its character to a varied geology and to the effects of climate and weathering over many millennia. Increasingly, man has played a part in this process, and today the modern landscape is almost entirely a product of human intervention.

The dominant lie of the land is from south-east to north-west; the direction of flow of the majority of rivers, and of many of its hills. Somerset is both cradled and intersected by a series of hills, which together with the Levels give it such a distinctive character. The highest land in the west rises above 500 metres in the Devonian sandstone and slate rocks of Exmoor, where the rainfall is highest and the predominantly acid soils are most suitable for cattle or sheep pasture. Eastwards lie the Brendon Hills, which are separated in turn from the Quantock Hills by a broad, fertile valley that links the equally fertile Vale of Taunton Deane to the south with the northern coastal plain. Most of west Somerset is characterised by red soils; on the uplands derived from Devonian rocks, while the more fertile lowlands are based primarily upon softer clays and shales of Permian and Triassic age. Clays and sands of the Cretaceous period form the Blackdown Hills, whose steep north-facing scarp overlooks the Vale of Taunton Deane along the county's southern border.

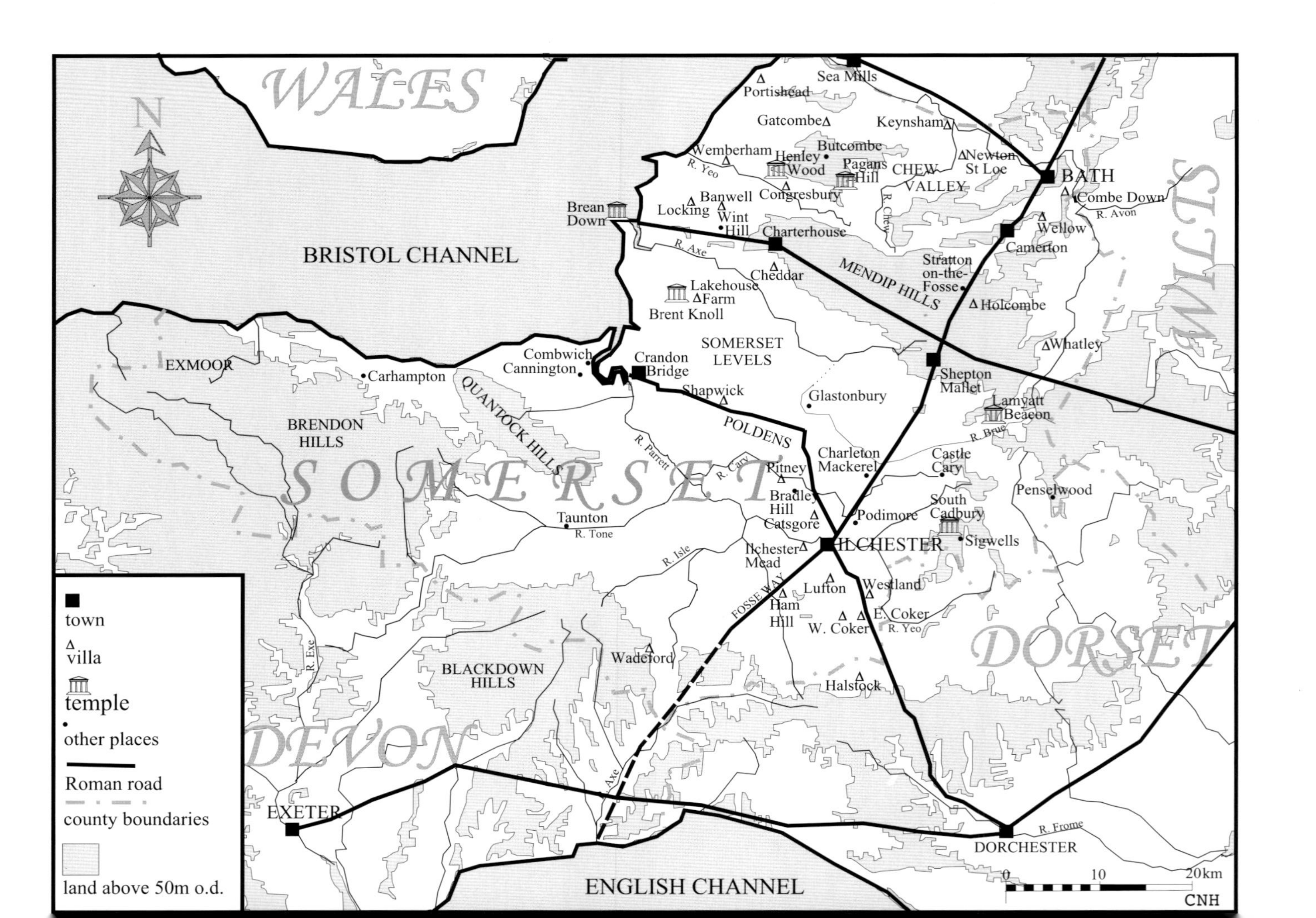
WALES
WILTS
SOMERSET
DORSET
DEVON
BRISTOL CHANNEL
ENGLISH CHANNEL
N
Sea Mills
Portishead
Gatcombe
Keynsham
Wemberham
R. Yeo
Henley Wood
Butcombe
Pagans Hill
CHEW VALLEY
Newton St Loe
BATH
Combe Down
R. Avon
Brean Down
Banwell
Locking
Wint Hill
Congresbury
R. Chew
Charterhouse
Wellow
Camerton
R. Axe
Cheddar
MENDIP HILLS
Stratton on-the-Fosse
Holcombe
Lakehouse Farm
Brent Knoll
Whatley
EXMOOR
Carhampton
Combwich
Cannington
Crandon Bridge
SOMERSET LEVELS
Shepton Mallet
Shapwick
Glastonbury
Lamyatt Beacon
R. Brue
BRENDON HILLS
QUANTOCK HILLS
R. Parrett
POLDENS
R. Cary
Pitney
Charleton Mackerel
Castle Cary
Penselwood
Bradley Hill
Catsgore
Podimore
South Cadbury
Taunton
R. Tone
ILCHESTER
Sigwells
Ilchester Mead
R. Isle
Lufton
Westland
FOSSE WAY
Ham Hill
W. Coker
E. Coker
R. Yeo
R. Exe
Wadeford
BLACKDOWN HILLS
Halstock
R. Axe
EXETER
DORCHESTER
R. Frome
0
10
20km
CNH
town
villa
temple
other places
Roman road
county boundaries
land above 50m o.d.

Above. The ramparts of an Iron Age hillfort on Brent Knoll probably contained a Roman temple, and overlook the Somerset Levels and the M5 motorway (top).

Opposite page. A map showing some of the principal sites in Roman Somerset.

From here the River Tone flows eastwards to join the River Parrett, its lower valley opening out into that extensive tract of lowland and fen country known collectively as the Somerset Levels. The Levels proper are characteristically flat, in parts lying just below sea level, and comprising areas of peat moor and soft alluvial clays. To the west they are bounded by the tidal estuaries and mudflats of the Bristol Channel, backed in many places by sand dunes. Further inland, isolated hills, promontories and ridges of higher ground, like the Polden Hills, Wedmore ridge, Brent Knoll, Nyland Hill, Glastonbury, or Burrow Mump interrupt the Levels. Though of no great height, some of these hills rise dramatically from their flat surroundings as islands of older and harder Jurassic and Triassic rocks.

To the north the Levels are bounded by the Mendip Hills, whose highest parts (200-300 metres) are Devonian and Carboniferous limestone and sandstone uplands. Often steep sided, the Mendips are something of a barrier between north Somerset and the rest of the county. A separate and smaller area of lowland fen – the North Somerset Levels – lies to the north, behind the Bristol Channel coast and skirted by further steep ridges and hills. Eastwards, the country becomes more

The Mendip Hills under snow, viewed from the top of Glastonbury Tor.

broken towards the Chew Valley, Radstock and Bath. Older rocks, including Coal measures, are overlain by the Jurassic clays and limestones that mark the southern edge of the Cotswold Hills around Bath.

Much of south and east Somerset is formed of Jurassic and Cretaceous rocks, occurring as a succession of clays, sands and soft limestones, and responsible for alternating clay vales, undulating ranges of hills and some deeply cut valleys. The more resistant limestone outcrops, as between Frome, Yeovil, and Crewkerne create the most prominent hills, and some of the most fertile soils in the county can be found in this broad tract of country. Many of the rivers that water the Somerset Levels originate from the rocks in this area, notably the Brue, Cary, Yeo, Parrett and Isle. The upper valleys of these rivers form a broad lowland vale between south-east Mendip and the Blackdown Hills, extending into the Vale of Taunton Deane to the west.

The Romano-British countryside was essentially a creation of its native Iron Age people and their forbears. The uplands of Exmoor, the Brendon and Quantock Hills were cleared early of their native woodland, their generally poor soils and high rainfall supporting extensive tracts of moorland and pasture, although many of the deeper valleys will have been densely wooded. Settlement, based principally upon a pastoral economy, will always have been sparse and widely scattered, and there was probably little change in its character or density from the later prehistoric period and throughout the time of Roman

Compton Dundon from Somerton; a south Somerset valley, overlooked by the hillfort (left) and the Polden Hills (right), was the location for several wealthy Roman villas.

administration. The pre-Roman Somerset Levels, north and south of the Mendip Hills, contained what were probably the most extensive tracts of natural vegetation and landscape within the county, though even they were already subject to a degree of human exploitation and modification. These wetland areas were to experience fundamental changes during the Roman period, although most of the islands and promontories of higher land had long been cleared and settled in prehistoric times.

The Mendip Hills were another region with a predominantly pastoral economy. Their higher reaches had long been converted to extensive downland pastures for grazing, although some steep slopes and the narrower valleys and ravines doubtless supported much semi-natural woodland. The country north and east of Mendip had been settled since the Neolithic period, and by Roman times was probably a relatively wealthy region of mixed arable and pastoral agriculture, with some tracts of woodland. Further south and east the woodlands became more extensive, notably in Bruton Forest and Selwood, occupying the clay vale and the Greensand escarpment along Somerset's eastern border. Much of this persisted until its clearance and settlement in medieval times.

South Somerset is a land of broad fertile valleys and rolling limestone hills. For the 2,500 years that divide the Late Bronze Age (1000 BC) from the early post-medieval period (AD 1500) it remained the wealthiest and most densely settled part of the county. Mixed farming was the basis for its power and prestige, seen initially in the great hillforts of the Iron Age, and subsequently in wealthy Roman estates. After Bath, Somerset's principal Roman town – Ilchester - was located at the heart of this region, through which ran the Fosse Way, one of the major arteries of Roman Britain.

GOVERNMENT

The Somerset conquered by Rome was split politically between three major indigenous tribal peoples: the Dumnonii to the west, the Durotriges in the centre, and the Dobunni to the north. None of these peoples may initially have welcomed Roman government; the Durotriges in particular, but Roman imperial policy was to govern her provinces through local participation and by retaining pre-existing political and economic structures. Thus, what was historically to become a single county, was shared between three administrative units based upon the original Iron Age tribes throughout the Roman period. These basic units of local government were known as *civitates* (effectively counties), administered from centres within each tribal region by the principal land-owning, and native-born aristocracy.

We have no contemporary maps of Roman Britain, but inscriptions, rare documents, and archaeological remains allow us to identify these centres, and to estimate the approximate boundaries of the *civitates*. To the west, the rather loose confederation of Dumnonians had their capital at Exeter (*Isca Dumnoniorum*), with the River Parrett as their eastern boundary. The *civitas* Durotrigum was governed from Dorchester (*Durnovaria*) in Dorset, its northern territory covering the Levels and south Somerset. The Mendip Hills and north Somerset lay within the lands of the Dobunni. Their capital was at Cirencester (*Corinium Dobunnorum*) in Gloucestershire; however, this region had always been distinct, and seems rather to have been incorporated by the Roman provincial government into the Civitas Belgarum, whose capital was Winchester.

A council or senate, known as the *ordo*, whose members were called *decurions*, governed the *civitates*. These were drawn from the former tribal aristocracy, and local chieftains. The *decurions* elected an executive *curia* and magistrates, annually in pairs, who would be responsible for such matters as local justice, public shows and religious festivals, public works (roads, water supply, buildings, etc.), local taxation, conducting a periodic census, and representing the *civitas* at the provincial council in London (until the third century). This was a constitution based essentially upon the city-state of Rome itself, and by taking advantage of the pre-existing native hierarchical system in this way Rome was able to consolidate its position in partnership with the native inhabitants, and encourage the rapid and successful integration of a new province into its empire.

Supreme authority was vested in the governor of the province of Britannia, responsible directly to the emperor for the effective running of the *civitates*, as well as for the military garrisons in Wales and the north. Alongside him was a *procurator*, whose responsibilities were primarily financial through maintenance of the imperial tax system. At the end of the second century the province was split into two, its southern half (*Britannia Superior*) including the Somerset *civitates*. Almost a century later a further subdivision into four under the emperor Diocletian, saw Somerset become part of the province of *Britannia Prima* (Wales and south-west England) with its capital at Cirencester. The *civitas* capitals played a key early role in fostering the ideals of Roman civilization and citizenship, although this was to change from the third century onwards, as the financial responsibilities of the *decurions* became more onerous and the nature of towns and society in general changed within the late Roman empire.

FOUR

Aquae Sulis – Roman Bath

At Bath, in the north-east corner of the county, is one of the premier sites of Roman Britain. Today, the city is renowned for its hot springs and Georgian elegance, but Bath (*Aquae Sulis*) was also a major Roman centre, famed both through Britain and the Empire. Its hot springs have been its fortune ever since the Romans first recognised their potential As in the Georgian and Regency periods, important and architecturally imposing buildings also graced the Roman city.

THE SETTING

Bath lies within the deep valley of the River Avon, where it cuts through the southern end of the Cotswold Hills. In a sharp bend on the north side of the river, three hot springs bubble up from a low promontory within a hundred metres or so of each other. The hottest – at 49 degrees celsius - is the Hot Bath spring, with the Cross Bath spring at 40 degrees celsius nearby. These flow together for a few hundred yards south-westwards to join the river. To the east the King's Bath spring is the most powerful, with a flow of nearly one third of a million gallons a day at 46 degrees celsius, making its way southwards in a separate shallow valley into the Avon.

These are almost the only hot springs known in Britain. Even before the Romans, their emergence, steaming and bubbling from the earth, must have been a great wonder to our prehistoric ancestors. Because their sources now lie deep beneath successive buildings and archaeological remains, we know little about their use before Roman times. Finds suggest that they were venerated during the later Iron Age, while flint tools indicate interest and activity around them for many thousands of years previously. The springs are no less impressive today; not least because we now know that their water has taken some 6,000 years to travel from the Mendip Hills – where it fell as rain – down several thousand metres into the earth's crust to be heated, before rising through the Carboniferous limestone rocks to emerge again at Bath.

Because of their unusual nature, the hot springs probably became the focus for religious veneration and ritual early on. The remains of Neolithic and Bronze Age monuments are relatively abundant around Bath, and by the Iron Age this was a populous region, as the remains of

A reconstruction of Roman Bath in its heyday; the walled precinct in the foreground, with the town and river crossing beyond.

settlements, field systems and local hillforts such as Bathampton Hill and Little Solsbury testify. As yet there is no evidence for prehistoric settlement close to the springs themselves, although excavations at the King's Bath spring suggest that some time in the late Iron Age it had been lined with wooden stakes to confine its edges, and that it was approached along a gravel causeway. Water – lakes and rivers, and in particular its sources in springs – featured prominently in Celtic religion, and Bath's hot springs were probably especially venerated; supplicants approaching them via the causeway through what was probably a mysterious wooded, steamy swamp, to make offerings like the 18 gold and silver Celtic coins which have been found in excavations here.

Although Bath's hot springs were well known before the arrival of the Romans, they were not the army's prime objective when subjugating the area. Less than one kilometre north of the springs was an important ford across the River Avon. At this point, now marked by the Cleveland Bridge, lay the junction and crossing point for two major Roman roads – the Fosse Way from north to south, and the road east from London and Silchester that continued west to the Severn Estuary at Sea Mills.

These roads were established during the early years of the Conquest, and there is strong evidence that a fort was built here to guard the river crossing. There are finds of military equipment, coins, pottery and other material, including tombstones, dating to the middle years of the first century AD following the Conquest in the area. But whether the fort was sited in Walcot or just across the river to the east in Bathwick, has yet to be established. The army undoubtedly appreciated the benefits of a local supply of naturally heated water, and may well have used it for bathing, although no evidence for their bathhouse has yet been found. The Bath garrison may have moved on from this area within twenty years or so of the Conquest, but it was surely their initial involvement and support that enabled the hot springs to be exploited by the new civil authorities. Gradually, a remarkable complex of ritual, religious and recreational buildings rose around them.

THE SACRED SPRING

Thanks to a series of archaeological excavations carried out over the past thirty years or so, as well as discoveries and records made in the eighteenth and nineteenth centuries, a great deal is now known of the layout and character of the buildings around the King's Bath spring in particular. Initially it was necessary to control the source of the sacred spring and the abundant flow of its waters; a task perhaps best suited to engineers in the Roman army. The first priority was to lower the water table and drain the swampy hollow around the springhead. This was achieved by building a great subterranean stone drain with an arched roof and wooden channel along its base. This was high enough to walk along, and was equipped with manholes for access to clean it out or for repairs. It still works to this day, carrying waste water down into the river. Once in operation, the drain lowered the water level around the spring and allowed the Roman engineers to build an artificial pool or reservoir to contain it. This itself was an ingenious structure, which commenced with the sinking of numerous, closely set oak piles around the spring. Around this a further ring of piles provided support for a massive stone-block wall which created a roughly oval reservoir pool. To make it waterproof the timber piles were sealed with puddled clay,

A reconstruction of the building of the reservoir around the sacred spring, Bath.

whilst the stone sides and part of the bottom was covered by lead sheeting. A thick ledge of concrete set with tiles then sealed the bottom step.

While all these works were in progress it was necessary to retain an opening near the bottom to allow the water to run into the great drain. Once completed the opening was plugged with timber and the pool filled up, excess water being drained from the top for distribution elsewhere. The bottom plug could still be removed to allow silt to be flushed out into the drain and keep the water relatively clear. At this time (late in the first century AD) it was open to the sky; but its steaming and bubbling dark green waters were doubtless an awesome spectacle for visitors. This sacred pool and spring thus became the focal point around which a remarkable complex of buildings developed.

THE TEMPLE OF SULIS MINERVA

Religion and ritual were very much at the heart of Roman Bath. In tandem with the remodelling and management of the King's Bath spring went the building of a temple. There are few temples known from Roman Britain which were modelled in the classical tradition, but such was the importance of the spring that an imposing classical temple was intended from the outset. Once the waters had been brought under control it was possible to lay out a rectangular precinct – a large colonnaded courtyard – which included the enclosed spring and its pool in the south-east corner. In the centre of the courtyard the original temple building comprised a podium, approximately fourteen metres long and nine metres wide, aligned virtually east-west, and built of concrete faced with stone blocks.

From the building fragments recovered in the course of various excavations, its east front can be reconstructed as having four fluted columns with plain bases and Corinthian capitals, rising to a height of about eight metres. These supported a frieze and architrave, the latter almost certainly bearing a monumental inscription, though little of these elements have survived. Above this was a triangular pediment, rather more of which has been found, framed by a highly decorated cornice.

This richly decorated pediment was dominated by a central gorgon's head – one of the most famous and dramatic pieces of sculpture from Roman Britain. In this representation the gorgon is male, almost certainly signifying the Celtic deity Sul or Sulis, already presiding over the springs as a sun god and/or water god. This famous head is set within a circular shield, supported by winged victories associated with symbols representing the classical god Minerva, thus epitomising the marriage between classical Roman and native deities so favoured within the Empire.

The temple platform stood well over a metre above the surrounding courtyard, and was probably approached by a short flight of stone steps along its east frontage. Very little of the temple interior is known, but the eighteenth century discovery of an almost life-size, gilded bronze head of Minerva *(see the frontispiece)* from a deep excavation beneath Stall Street, almost certainly belonged to the main cult statue of the goddess standing within the temple. The east exterior of the building was fronted by an area of flagstone paving, at the centre of which stood a large square, sacrificial altar. This was positioned centrally on the east-

A re-assembly of the east front pediment from the temple of Sulis Minerva, with the gorgon's head – thought to be a representation of the god Sulis.

west axis of the temple, but was also visible on a north-south axis across the sacred spring pool from the baths. Enough of the altar survives to reconstruct it as a square structure of stone blocks, with a smoothed and slightly dished upper surface upon which animal sacrifices would be laid. At its four corners were pairs of sculpture depicting classical gods, including Hercules, Jupiter, and perhaps Apollo or Orpheus.

The four-column east front of the later-first-century temple probably gave access via a narrow open porch to an enclosed room, known as the *cella*, where statues and dedications were kept and certain rituals took place. These parts of the building have yet to be excavated, but towards the end of the second century the temple was enlarged to almost twice its original size. This involved building a corridor around the outside of the first temple (which was probably left intact), and the erection of a new east façade. The original columns and pediment would still have been visible, but were now flanked on either side by shrines – probably both enclosed rooms, and a new set of stone steps approached from the altar and courtyard to the west. This modified building was now more like the traditional Romano-Celtic style of temple built widely throughout the western provinces of the Empire, examples of which have been discovered and excavated elsewhere in Somerset (see chapter 8). Few others were so grand, and this temple continued to be used throughout the third and fourth centuries, and probably into the fifth.

The expansion and remodelling of the temple was doubtless a reflection of the fame and popularity that the shrine soon achieved throughout Britain, and further afield. During the second century the precinct was enclosed by a plain outer wall on three sides, against the inside of which was later added a roofed colonnade. Perhaps as part of these works the sacred spring pool was now enclosed and roofed over. The height of the reservoir walls was increased and a large, rectangular stone building erected around it, with a great arched vaulted roof. In time, large fragments of the roof fell into the reservoir, preserving many details of its construction. Within this room, in the warm and steamy half-light, the sacred spring and pool would have seemed even more

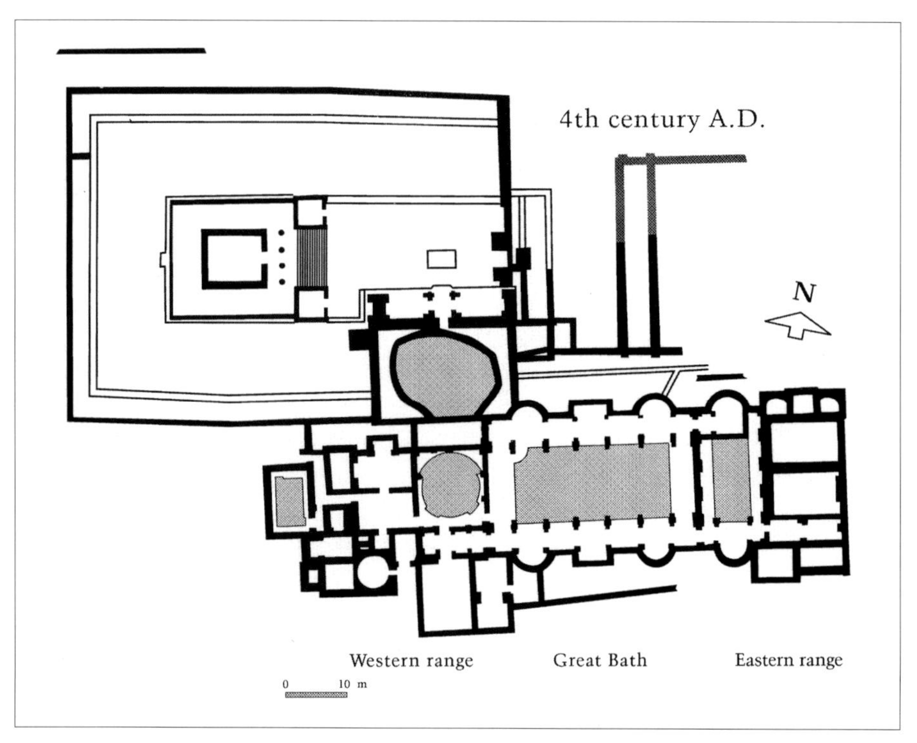

A general plan of the known temple and baths complex.

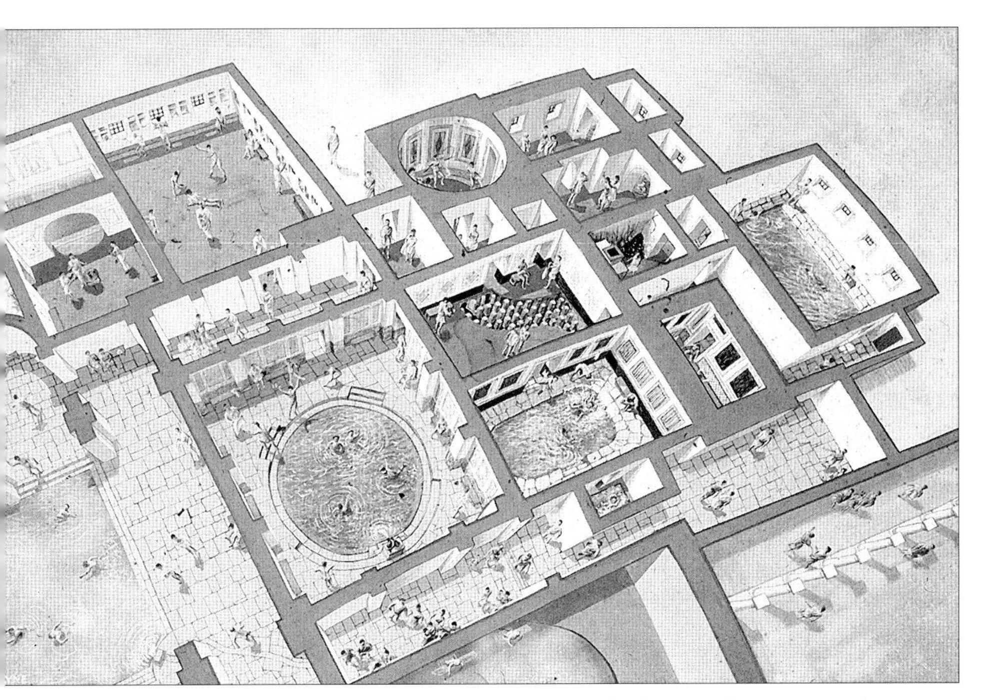

A reconstruction of the west end of the Roman baths complex as it may have looked in the third century, showing part of the great bath (bottom left) and suites of bathing, changing and treatment rooms.

mysterious. The walls may have been decorated and there were probably statues and altars placed around, some apparently upon plinths within the pool. A door gave entry from the precinct, but most supplicants and visitors will have viewed the pool from the baths, through openings in the south wall of the reservoir building.

THE GREAT BATHS

The discovery and interpretation of the remains of the Roman temple and its precinct has only taken place recently. For much of its history, Bath's reputation has rested on its hot baths. These were probably established during the Middle Ages, and are popularly known as the King's Bath, the Cross Bath and the Hot Bath. All three were preceded by Roman establishments. The largest and most elaborate lay beneath the King's Bath and was built as an integral part of the sacred spring and temple complex. They were rediscovered during the eighteenth-century redevelopment of the city, but were not opened up until later in the nineteenth century, when the Great Bath, which forms a centrepiece of the present museum, was exposed and partly restored. More recent archaeological investigations have uncovered further portions of the baths and new information about how they operated.

The baths were laid out originally at the same time as the temple precinct and sacred spring, towards the end of the first century AD. Effectively they form the south side of the precinct, massively built in stone on an east-west axis, and occupying an area almost eighty metres long and over thirty metres wide. The original design was for three basic units; the great bath to the east, a central hall, and a smaller bath suite to the west. The central hall had a cold bath at its south end, adjacent to what was probably the main entrance. At the north end three open archways gave a view over the sacred spring and into the temple precinct. The hall was the cold room (*frigidarium*), where bathers undressed. Turning left, they entered a suite of rooms that operated rather like a Turkish bath, going first into a warm dry room (*tepidarium*), before passing on to a much hotter room (*caldarium*). These rooms were heated by hot air supplied from beneath the floor (a *hypocaust*), and from tile flues set into the walls. From the *caldarium* the bather could return via the cooler *tepidarium* to take a cold bath at the end of the hall, or alternatively cross to the right and enter the warm baths.

The warm bath suite, fed directly from the sacred spring, was undoubtedly one of the wonders of Roman Britain. Even today, the great bath is an impressive sight, although only the bath itself and its lower surrounds survive. Originally, it lay within an aisled hall, flanked on either side by corridors, with recesses in their outer walls in which bathers could sit and rest. A continuous open arcade, the bases for which still survive, separated the corridors from the bath. The bath itself is one-and-a-half metres deep, twenty-two metres long and almost nine metres wide, with a continuous run of steps for entry around all four sides. These and the floor of the bath were lined with lead, although only the sheets on the bottom survive today. A fountain and perhaps some statuary were set in the centre of the north side of the bath. Water entered via a lead pipe from the sacred spring to the north-west, and could be drained out for purposes of cleaning and maintenance.

A flagstone pavement, most of which survives intact, surrounded the bath. Debris recovered during the nineteenth-century clearance of the great bath suggests that the great hall would have had a simple but impressive interior, its vaulted roof rising thirteen metres or more above the floor, and with an upper arcade which would have had openings to allow in light from above. A partition divided the east end of the hall from a smaller room that housed a separate and smaller warm bath. First discovered in the eighteenth century, this is known as the Lucas Bath, approximately thirteen by six metres, aligned approximately north-south across the width of the hall and fed by an overflow from the great bath. Beyond lay a slightly smaller bath, also fed by an overflow,

View of the Great Bath empty of water, showing its original lead-lined bottom.

and almost filling another room at the eastern extremity of the hall.

Such was the undoubted popularity of the baths that alterations and additions were soon required; a process which probably began early in the second century and continued on well into the fourth century, and possibly beyond. Initially, these works involved extending the facilities at both the east and west ends of the baths to provide more changing and bathing rooms. By the end of the second century a more fundamental rebuilding was required, which involved re-roofing the whole establishment with a barrel vault and extensions at both ends. Even more elaborate modifications and the rebuilding of the heated rooms followed thereafter, including clear evidence for the provision of curative immersion baths.

Further modifications and repairs seem to have continued through the fourth century, although precise dating is often difficult. Only the great bath seems to have been maintained virtually unaltered throughout the centuries, but towards the end of its life the baths suffered increasingly from flooding, probably because its drainage system was neglected. Eventually this forced its abandonment, possibly early in the fifth century, and thereafter the site reverted back to a marsh.

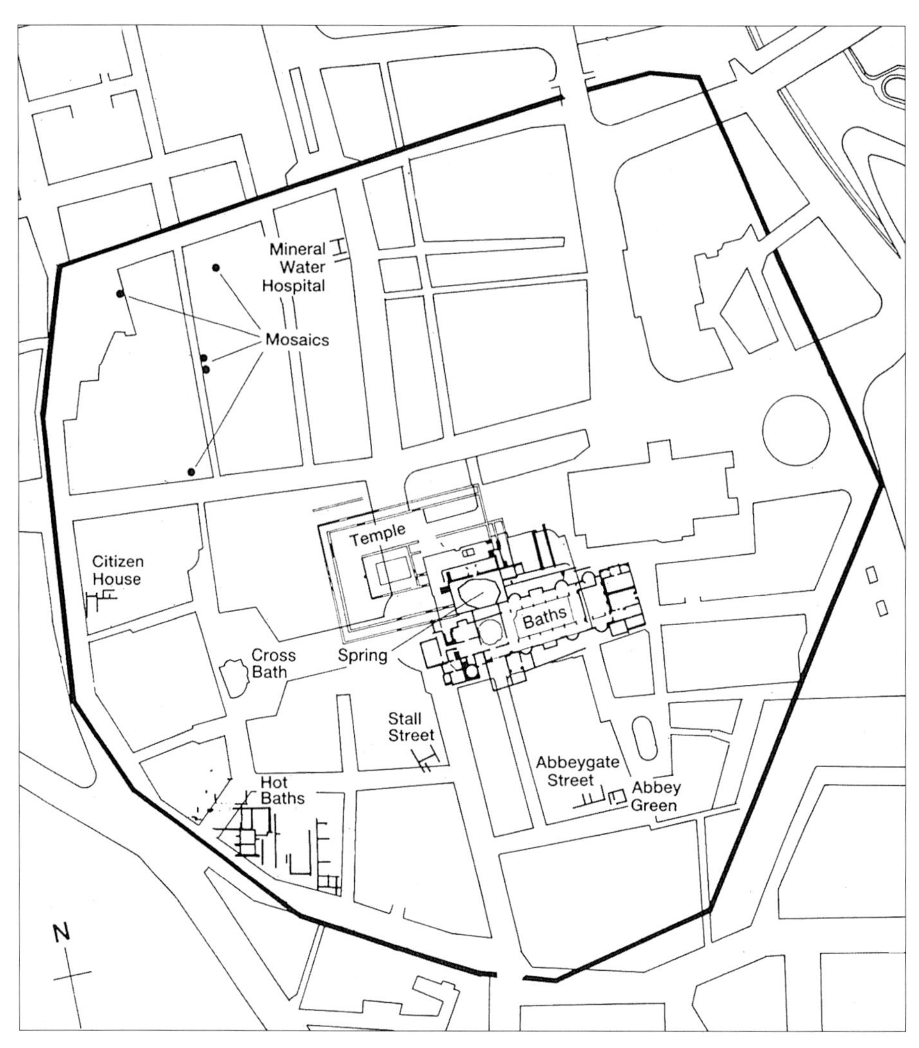

The walled precinct; a simplified plan of Roman remains superimposed upon the modern streets of Bath.

THE WALLED PRECINCT

The baths and temple complex lie at the heart of a walled precinct, but when was this wall built, what did it represent, and what else lay within its orbit? Necessarily limited opportunities for archaeological investigation of the defences of *Aquae Sulis* suggest that an area of approximately nine hectares was first enclosed by a rampart and ditch around the end of the second century, before its replacement by a stone wall at the beginning of the fourth century. This is a sequence recognised widely within other towns of Roman Britain, and in Somerset there is almost identical evidence at Ilchester (Chapter 5). The precise significance of these defences in Britain is still not fully understood,

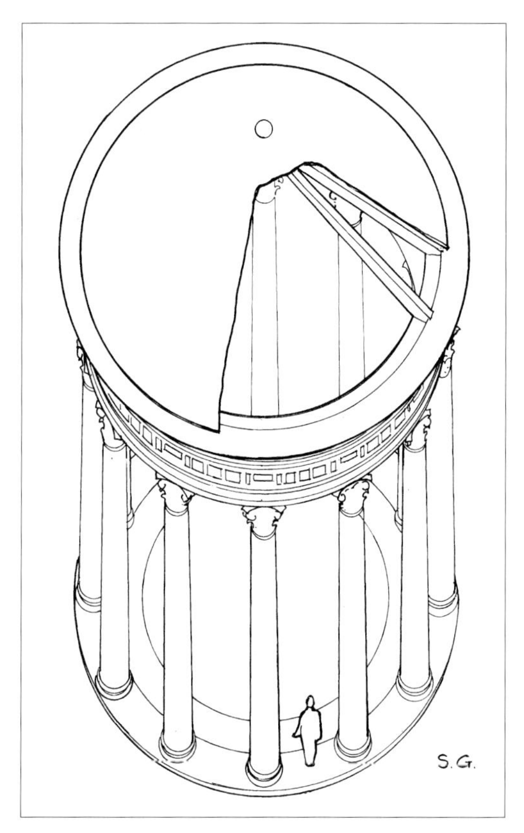

A suggested reconstruction of the Hadriannic tholos.

although the later provision of walls was undoubtedly a guarantee of greater security for the more important centres in the troubled times of the later fourth and early fifth centuries. Towns with local administrative status, notably the *civitas* capitals such as Dorchester, Exeter or Cirencester, were certainly enclosed in this manner, and Ilchester may have been among them, but what was the status of Bath?

The long history of discovery and investigation within the temple and baths complex has given us quite a detailed picture of this area, but what else lay within the walls? Immediately to the north-east lies the great medieval church of Bath Abbey, where discoveries made close to its west front suggest the presence of another monumental Roman building. It has been suggested that building foundations here represent the south-west corner of another temple, which would have been sited beneath what is now the abbey church. Architectural fragments also suggest the nearby presence of an elaborate circular building, which has been interpreted as a *tholos*. This was an open structure of perhaps twelve columns with a roof, approximately nine metres in diameter and over seven metres high. Although its exact site is unknown, a location on the same axis as the temple of Sulis Minerva would be appropriate, whose proportions it appears to mirror. The Bath *tholos* is so far unique in Roman Britain. Stylistically it is of the early second century, and may have been built at the instigation of the emperor Hadrian during his visit to Britain in AD 122.

An even more massive public building may have stood just to the north of the temple, although only a few fragments have been found. The ground rises quite steeply here, making it a natural site for a theatre to stage religious performances. Theatres were commonly included within major religious complexes, and there are other examples in Roman Britain – as at Gosbecks near Colchester, or Frilford in Oxfordshire.

The two other hot springs at Bath lie close by, to the south-west of the King's Bath spring and still within the town walls. The Cross Bath spring was enclosed by an oval stone wall, with a sluice to the south which channelled its overflow along a large drain in the direction of the Hot Baths spring. This suggests an arrangement similar to the reservoir pool created at the King's Bath spring, where visitors might have come to a pool and made offerings. It is not clear how the Hot Baths spring was enclosed, but altars dedicated to Sulis Minerva and to Diana, as well as numerous coins found here, suggests that it was also venerated. Discoveries and records made in the nineteenth century, just to the south of the Hot Baths spring, demonstrate the presence there of another major public baths complex, doubtless supplied by the spring.

Elsewhere within the walls discoveries have been more piecemeal, but remains of further buildings are widespread, and where detailed excavations have been possible show that other parts of the town were being developed from the later first century. Timber seems to have been widely used for buildings at first, but by the second century these were being replaced in stone and mortar. As time went on the density of development increased, particularly after the defences were built, although it was not long before the first phase of earthen bank and ditch began to be encroached upon. In the fourth century the walls provided a more permanent barrier, although this seems to have been the period of maximum growth and prosperity for *Aquae Sulis*.

Some of the remains found within the walls may represent other public buildings, but there was also a large resident population. So important a shrine would have been served by priests and officials, as well as by servants and workers, including slaves. Many of these will have lived close by the temples, baths, and their other places of work. Artisans and shopkeepers, serving the visitors and supplicants, had premises here, in many cases living in them. Some building remains may be of hostels or guesthouses, where visitors would have stayed. Finally, the quality and sophistication of some buildings might be due to their ownership by wealthy local landowners or new immigrants building urban villas.

WITHOUT THE WALLS

There was much more to Roman Bath than the relatively small core of public buildings centred upon the sacred springs, and the ancillary activities associated with them contained within the walls. Indeed, the walls might be seen better as the *temenos* or enclosure for a sacred precinct, rather than demarcating a town proper. Unlike most towns in Roman Britain, the main road system appears to bypass this centre. The river crossing, a few hundred metres to the north, was the objective for both the Fosse Way and the road from London, which ends on the Severn Estuary at Sea Mills. This crossing was originally a ford, which may later have been bridged, and it soon became a second focus for settlement.

It was the army that first took advantage of this junction of river and road crossings, but it was the nearby sacred springs, temples and public facilities that encouraged further growth. Apart from on both banks at the actual crossing point of the River Avon, the main area of development was uphill to the west, and southwards along the street which linked the crossing with the walled precinct, in the area now known as Walcot.

Archaeological remains have often only come to light in a haphazard fashion, usually as a result of new development in what is now a heavily built-up part of the city. It is now clear that the scale of Roman development here probably exceeded that of the walled town. Some wealthy town houses have been located, with mosaic floors, painted walls and heated rooms, but this part of Bath was probably the principal centre for manufacturing and trade. Many buildings will have been tenements facing onto the main road frontages, and were home to the shopkeepers and artisans who supplied the needs of the steady stream of visitors to the baths and sacred shrines, as well as people from the surrounding countryside, for whom Bath was their market centre. On the fringes of the built-up areas and usually close to the roads, was where most of the townspeople, as well as some of the visitors, were buried. Burial within Roman towns was normally a forbidden activity, but cemeteries have been identified along all the major routes into Bath, to the north, south, west, and across the river to the east in Bathwick.

There is little doubt that in its heyday Bath was the largest town in Somerset, as well as the centre for parts of what are now Gloucestershire and Wiltshire. Under the Roman system of local government it may have been included within the *civitas* of the Belgae, whose main centre was at

Winchester. However, on the eve of the Roman Conquest this area probably lay within the territory of the Dobunni, whose *civitas* capital was Cirencester. There is still uncertainty about its political affiliations, but Bath almost certainly had a local administrative role. This was a wealthy area, as the great concentration of country estates and their villas around the town testifies. Bath may have been governed by the owners of such estates, many of them of native stock, and probably functioned both as a centre for the collection of taxes and as an official posting station (the *cursus publicus*), particularly later in its life.

THE PEOPLE

Bath is rightly famed as one of the most spectacular sites of Roman Britain, but no less fascinating is the window it provides us into the lives of its inhabitants and visitors. *Aquae Sulis* soon gained a reputation as a great religious shrine and centre for healing. This brought visitors from many parts of the Empire, as well as from all over Britain. Many will have come to make offerings at the springs and temple, others to benefit from the healing properties of the waters. Activities such as these, as well as the rituals, attracted inscriptions and dedications. Bath has one of the greatest concentrations of contemporary written material surviving from Roman Britain, both naming individuals and giving us a valuable insight into the daily life and preoccupations of its citizens.

Writing normally only survives on durable material, wood, paper or parchment having long since perished. Bath has long been famed for its fine building stone, prompting remarkable buildings and sculpture, and also providing a canvas for inscriptions. Relatively few of the public inscriptions and dedications placed on buildings like the main cult temple or the baths have survived, although many of a more personal nature have been recovered and can be seen in the Roman Baths Museum today.

Some of the earliest were tombstones set up by soldiers, who may have been stationed at the fort thought to lie close to the river crossing. These include two soldiers of the Twentieth Legion – Marcus Valerius Latinus and Antigonus, and a Spanish cavalryman – Lucius Vitellius Tancinus – who died at the age of 46. Others came here as visitors or to live after their retirement from military service. Two serving soldiers from France died in their twenties, from wounds or illness – Julius Vitalis an armourer of the Twentieth Legion, and Gaius Murrius Modestus of the Second Legion. Others probably came to settle in or around Bath on their retirement, by which time they would have been granted Roman citizenship and become relatively wealthy members of society. One was Marcus Aufidius Maximus, a centurion of the Sixth Legion, who had two altars erected for him within the temple precinct by

The tombstone of Julius Vitalis, an armourer of the Twentieth Legion from Gallia Belgica (Belgium).

two of his freed slaves – perhaps in gratitude. Another centurion was Gaius Curiatius Saturninus of the Second Legion, who set up an altar at the Cross Bath spring. Of particular interest is the altar dedicated by the centurion Gaius Severius Emeritus, recording his restoration of a shrine 'wrecked by insolent hands' – an early instance of Christian iconoclasm in the fourth century perhaps? Emeritus identified himself as 'centurion in charge of this region', which implies his status as the administrator of a local imperial estate – possibly that centred on the nearby settlement at Combe Down, which is identified by another inscription from that site.

Two inscriptions record servants of the temple of Sulis Minerva. Gaius Calpurnius Receptus was a priest who died at the age of 75, and was remembered on a tombstone set up by his wife Calpurnia Trifosa, another freed slave. Within the temple precinct was a statue base dedicated by Lucius Marcius Memor – an *augur* – a senior official responsible for interpreting animal sacrifices and other omens. Claudius Ligur and Gaius Protacius are two other names connected with restoration works in the temple, although possibly just as wealthy citizens of Bath.

Most of the visitors to the temple, springs and baths complex will have come as supplicants, seeking health, fortune, or support from the gods. Dedications in gratitude or expectation of favours will have been common, and include that from Tiberius Claudius Sollemnis on white Italian marble, and altars dedicated to Sulis Minerva by Quintus Pompeius Anicetus and by Sulinus son of Maturus. Stone inscriptions were almost invariably commissioned by the wealthier members of society. The identities of those who made their living from the visitors are more rarely known, although they include two stonemasons – Priscus son of Toutius from the Chartres region of France, and Sulinus son of Brucetius, whose workshop may have been in Cirencester – and a doctor (doubtless one of many), whose name Tiberius Junianus is recorded on his seal.

Perhaps the largest recorded group of names (over one hundred) come from the lead plaques, or curse tablets, which were thrown into the sacred spring as part of dedicatory rituals. These were effectively prayers to the god or goddess, requesting favours, restitution of wrongs or the resolution of disputes, more often than not when property had been stolen or some harm done to the supplicant. Typical is the following: 'Docilianus son of Brucerus to the most holy goddess Sulis. I curse him who has stolen my hooded cloak, whether man or woman, slave or free, that the goddess Sulis inflicts death upon . . . (?) . . . not allow him sleep or children now and in the future, until he has brought my cloak to the temple of her divinity'.

Another appears to record a family dispute: 'Uricalus, Docilosa his wife, Docilis his son and Docilina, Decentinus his brother, Alogiosa: the names of those who have sworn at the spring of the goddess Sulis on the 12th April. Whosoever there has perjured himself you are to make him pay for it to the goddess Sulis in his own blood'. Theft, retribution, and the naming of suspects are common themes: 'I have given to the goddess Sulis, the six silver pieces which I have lost. It is for the goddess to extract it from the debtors written below.' What may have been another curse from the same person – Annianus – listed 18 possible suspects, covering all possibilities: 'Whether pagan or Christian, whosoever, whether man or woman, whether boy or girl, whether slave or free, has stolen from me, Annianus, in the morning, six silver pieces from my purse...'.

Many of these invocations seem to have a common formula, and were probably written in the temple precinct by scribes in exchange for a fee. As well as providing glimpses of the daily lives and concerns of both citizens and visitors to Bath, they provide us with names, many of which will have been common among the Romano-British population of

Pewter 'curse' tablets from the sacred spring, including one recording a vow made there by the family of Uricalus (bottom left).

Somerset. Some were Latin, like Annianus, Decentius, Dracontias, Innocentius, Simplicius, Vitorina or Minervina, but there were also many Celtic names, such as Belator, Cunomolius, Uricalus, Cunitius, Senovara or Surilla. This, and the identification of several as slaves, suggests that these inscriptions are more representative of the lower orders of society.

In addition to these prayers or curses, other objects were thrown into the sacred spring. In effect, they were committed to the goddess as gifts or sacrifices in exchange for assistance from the deity. Coins were perhaps the most common, and many thousands have been recovered from the silts, including some of gold and silver, and spanning the whole period of Roman administration from the first to the end of the fourth century. Personal objects such as jewellery, brooches, rings and gemstones have been recovered, as well as metal vessels of bronze, pewter and sometimes silver. Some of the cups and bowls were inscribed with dedications to the goddess, Sulis Minerva, and may have been made especially to be sold and then deposited in the spring. Even to this day we throw coins and other items into wells, springs or fountains 'for luck', suggesting perhaps that in our hopes and fears we are little different to our ancestors living almost two thousand years ago in Roman Britain.

FIVE

Ilchester and the Lendinienses

There could scarcely be a greater contrast today between the cosmopolitan bustle of Bath and the sleepy town that is Ilchester. Although lying astride the Fosse Way. its equally important modern successor, the A303, now bypasses the town. The Fosse Way links Bath and Ilchester, from where it crosses the River Yeo to skirt the poorly drained valleys of the Yeo, Parrett and Isle, on its journey to Exeter and the South West. Despite its relatively modest status today, Ilchester lay towards the centre of that part of the Durotrigan *civitas* within Somerset and has some claim to administrative importance rivalling the *civitas* capital at Dorchester.

ORIGINS

Ilchester had already acquired a special status in the late Iron Age when a large embanked enclosure was built in the meadows just south of the later town. Although we have only a limited understanding of this site and its function, it evidently represents some move towards social and political centralisation within the northern (Somerset) Durotriges, thus probably influencing both the location and suspected status of its Roman successor. Ilchester itself was positioned on a small island of gravel within the broad floodplain of the River Yeo, and at a crossing of the river. This crossing was used by the army for the route of the Fosse Way, and possibly as the site of a fort, during the first years of military conquest and occupation. So far, the evidence for what may have been a garrison is no more than a set of crop marks on the north bank of the river. Later, however, a larger fort was established on the south bank, astride the Fosse Way.

Archaeological excavations at Ilchester have established that this second fort covered approximately seven hectares and lay centrally beneath the later town. All four sides have been located, but virtually nothing is known of its interior. Remains of a clay bank reinforced with turves and timber have been found, fronted by a V-profiled ditch up to two metres deep. On the east side the defences comprised a pair of parallel ditches separated by a timber palisade, although the inner defensive bank had been levelled and built over. Outside the fort to the west, pits dug to extract gravel were infilled with rubbish disposed of

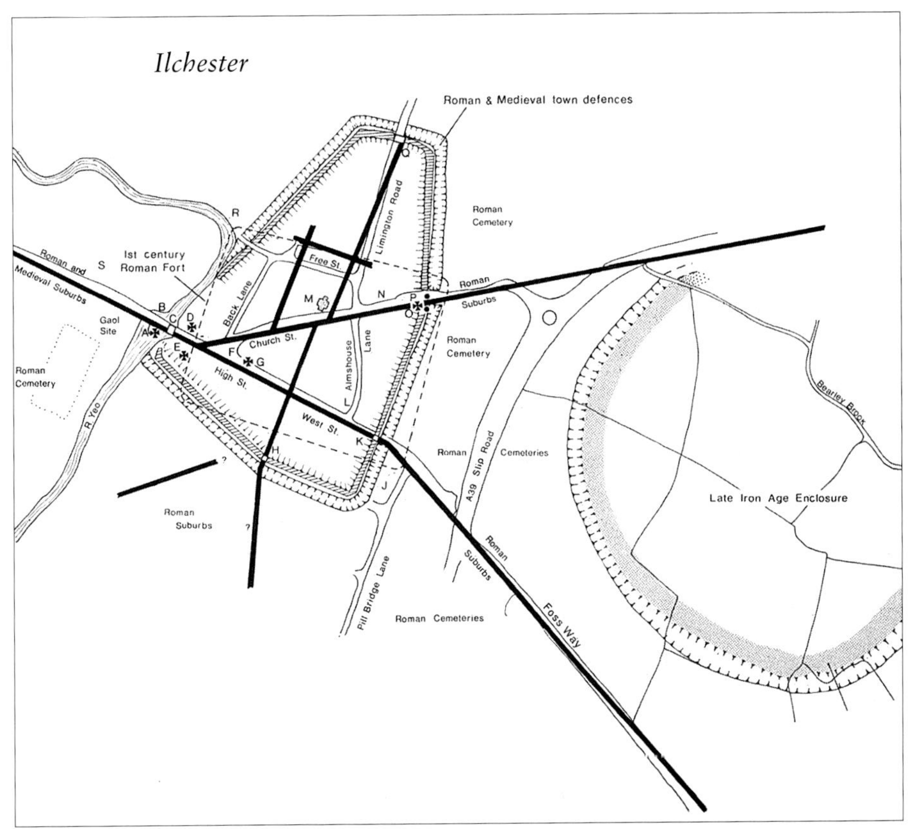

Roman Ilchester. A plan showing the location of the town, fort site and Iron Age *oppidum*.

when the fort went out of use. Along the Fosse Way to the south-west were the remains of timber-framed buildings set within a ditched enclosure. These may have been part of a depot located outside the south-west gate of the fort, or a roadside civil settlement (known as a *vicus*) attracted by the presence of a substantial army garrison.

It has been suggested that this fort may have been a response to unrest in the west at the time of the Boudiccan revolt in AD 60 (see chapter 2). The dating evidence available from finds of pottery, coins and other metalwork suggests its construction around that time, and an occupation that may not have lasted for much more than ten years. To some extent the military may have been responsible for encouraging the subsequent development of a town at Ilchester through their initial use of the site, along with the crossing point of the river by the Fosse Way, and its evident pre-Roman importance. Our knowledge of the early development of the town is still sparse, although the Roman fort remains seem to have been deliberately levelled and quickly built over before the end of the first century. The initial hostility of the Durotriges

Ilchester in the mid-20th century; an aerial view north along the Fosse Way. The walled area of the Roman town lies beneath the modern settlement.

to Roman rule, possibly continuing for a generation, may at first have inhibited the process of Romanisation in this part of Somerset and thus of Ilchester's development, but any such check will have been short-lived.

STATUS

Ilchester may be one of the oldest continuously inhabited places in Somerset, because of which opportunities for archaeological excavation have been limited. The activities of its more recent inhabitants have often disturbed the remains of its earlier occupants. Nevertheless, it has been possible to build up a picture of the Roman town by piecing together evidence from small excavations and discoveries made here over the past half century or so.

No inscription or other writing has ever been found at Ilchester which records its original name, however, the name '*Lindinis*' is recorded in a late Roman document known as the 'Ravenna Cosmography'. Furthermore, two inscriptions found at Hadrian's Wall record the presence of a contingent of workers from the *civitas* of the 'Durotriges

Two inscriptions on stones from Hadrian's Wall which refer to Ilchester – the *Civitas Durotrigum Lendiniensium* – some of whose citizens may have been conscripted to help with its repair in the third century.

Lendinienses' who helped repair and rebuild the wall – probably in the early third century. These were not from *Durnovaria* (Dorchester), but evidently from the northern part of the Durotrigan *civitas*. From these fragments of evidence the Roman name of *Lendiniae* has been proposed for Ilchester.

The building inscriptions from Hadrian's Wall have a further implication. Their attribution to the 'civitas' of the Durotriges of Lendiniae suggests that this was a separate *civitas* to that of the Dorchester Durotriges. This division may have come about sometime later, possibly during the second century. It has been suggested that *Lendiniae/Lindinis* means 'marsh' or 'little marsh', a name appropriate not only to Ilchester's site, but perhaps also to the people of this region, centred in and around the Somerset Levels – 'the people of the marshlands' perhaps?

The native pre-Roman Durotriges of Somerset probably regarded themselves as quite distinct from their Dorset cousins, a distinction that could have been reinforced under the Roman administration. The evidence for this enhanced status has yet to be demonstrated at Ilchester itself, but, as we shall see, the town lay within a particularly wealthy region, surrounded by a concentration of villa-based estates whose owners could well have served as *decurions* in the *civitas* government. Thus, Ilchester's claim to be the capital of a newly created *civitas Durotrigum Lendiniensium* seems to be strongly based.

URBAN LIFE

What was life like in *Lendiniae*? Despite the restrictions upon archaeological excavations in the town today, we can learn a lot by comparing discoveries made here with evidence from other Roman towns. Ilchester grew up around the crossing of the River Yeo and at the intersection of two major roads – The Fosse Way and the Dorchester Road on the south bank of the river. Another important road ran north-west along the Polden Hills to the Bristol Channel. No less vital was the river as a means of communication, particularly downstream to the River Parrett, the Levels, and ultimately to the sea. Looking at the twisting and often shallow course of the river today this is hard to imagine, but even in the nineteenth century coal barges unloaded at Pill Bridge, little more than a mile west of the town. The River Parrett is still tidal today up as far as Langport, about five miles downstream, and there is evidence that the Roman's straightened a stretch of the River Yeo above its crossing at Ilchester.

Apart from the two intersecting main roads within the town, we only have hints of other streets, although enough has been discovered to suggest that some sort of grid existed. The streets were surfaced with

Fragments of a decorated mosaic floor surviving from a building behind Limington Road, within the walls of Ilchester.

gravel and stone cobbles, their successive repair sometimes resulting in accumulations over one metre deep. As we find in towns today, buildings were set close together with their frontages onto the street, and sometimes with yards or small gardens behind. Few complete building plans have been found, and the best preserved were those of stone. Although Ilchester lies in the bottom of a valley, it has good sources of building stone nearby – especially Lias limestone and Ham Hill stone – both of which were used widely for building and roofing. Stone was used more extensively as Ilchester prospered and grew, although many of its earliest buildings were of timber, whose remains are often more difficult to detect.

We still have only a fragmentary town plan of *Lendiniae*, but it is clear that within a small built-up area of around 25 hectares there were a high proportion of relatively substantial houses. Many of these seem to have lined the main thoroughfares, and are distinguished by the presence of decorated mosaic floors, painted wall plaster, and a more spacious layout of rooms. Around thirty tessellated pavements are documented in Ilchester. One group was associated with an extensive building complex at Ivel House, close to the river crossing and occupying one side of what may have been a market place at the

Dorchester Road/ Fosse Way junction. Another large house with mosaic floors has been partly excavated behind Limington Road, not far from the town's former east gate. Further fragments of mosaic floors have come to light along the main road street frontages of the Fosse Way and the Dorchester Road. Houses such as these will have belonged to wealthy owners; in many instances the town houses of local landowners (the *decurions* of the *civitas*), otherwise represented by villa estates in the region.

Less sophisticated, but perhaps more common, were smaller tenement houses built closely together along the street frontages. Only one complete example has so far been excavated – behind Free Street in an area of gridded backstreets. It comprised a strip of three ground-floor rooms on a street corner, which probably combined as shop, workshop and living quarters (the latter on an upper floor?). Such premises are widely known in towns throughout the Empire, and are where the majority of Ilchester's citizens probably lived. Although it is unclear what trades were practised here, the building was first laid out towards the end of the first century over the levelled remains of the fort, and continued with some modifications into the fourth century.

One distinguishing feature of *civitas* capitals is public buildings, none of which have so far been traced at Ilchester. Among them would be a *basilica* (town hall), where the governing *ordo* met, local justice was dispensed, and accommodation was provided for various officials and civil servants. Frequently, the *basilica* was combined with a *forum* (market place), where shops, offices and sometimes temples were set around a large open courtyard. Many towns had large public baths, as have been excavated in Dorchester. Some had theatres or amphitheatres, and there may have been an official posting station known as a *mansio*.

The apparent absence of a *forum* or *basilica* could weaken Ilchester's claim for *civitas* status. What may be the site of one major public building is hinted at by occasional discoveries of large building foundations beneath and around the later medieval church of St Mary Major, but the opportunities for further excavation here are minimal.

By comparison with the other *civitas* capitals and major towns of Roman Britain, Ilchester was one of the smallest, but all the evidence recovered so far suggests a thriving and relatively prosperous community for much of its existence. Apart from its official functions (local government, judicial, tax collection, and probably housing an imperial posting station), Ilchester was an important market centre. From the surrounding countryside will have come farmers and villagers, as well as the wealthier landowners and their families, bringing their produce to exchange for products such as wine and oils, clothing, ornaments and jewellery, tools and implements, pottery, glass, etc., as

A selection of third and fourth century Roman coins found at Ilchester.

Black burnished Roman pottery from excavations within the town.

Northover (bottom) linked by the Fosse Way to Ilchester (top). The Roman cemetery lies mainly within the triangular walled area in the centre.

well as to pay their taxes. Within the town, shops and workshops would have been busy supplying both their fellow townsfolk and visitors, some of whom would have come from elsewhere in Britain as well as further afield within the Empire, by means of the roads or rivers.

SUBURBAN LIFE

One piece of evidence to support Ilchester's claim to *civitas* status is what appears to be the deliberate layout of a street grid at its heart. Development was not, however, restricted to this area, later to be enclosed by defences. As the town prospered there was growing pressure to expand, and the main roads out became the focus for suburban development. The most important suburb lay across the river to the north, flanking the Fosse Way for several hundred metres. This area is now occupied by the former medieval settlement of Northover (today part of Ilchester) and thus our knowledge of the Roman suburb beneath is slight. Both stone and timber buildings probably lined the street frontage, perhaps occupying more spacious plots than in the town itself. Trades such as butchery, tanning or metalworking would have been best sited here, and there is evidence for pottery manufacture at one location. Roman Northover appears to have developed northwards about as far as the medieval church of St Andrew, but its best known feature was the presence of a large cemetery on the west side of the main road.

In the Roman world burial was normally forbidden within dwelling areas, although such restrictions were not always adhered to, particularly in rural areas. The rules were more strictly applied in towns, where space would in any case have been limited, and roadside locations on the edge of towns became favoured sites for cemeteries. The Northover cemetery lies behind the Roman suburbs and largely beyond the bounds of later development – thus ensuring its relatively intact survival. Chance discoveries and some excavation enable us to estimate that at least 1500 of Ilchester's citizens were buried here. Many were buried in shrouds or wooden coffins, but some of the town's wealthier inhabitants could afford lead or stone coffins, and possibly mausolea. Most of the burials seem to date to the fourth century, although the cemetery could have a much earlier origin. Cremation was the more usual burial rite in the Roman world until the third century, but few have yet been discovered at Ilchester.

A Roman burial seen before its excavation, within a lead coffin and stone sarcophagus, Northover cemetery.

The continuation of the Fosse Way south of Ilchester provided the focus for another extensive roadside suburb, parts of which still lie beyond the bounds of more modern development. The construction of Ilchester's bypass in the 1970s provided the opportunity for large-scale archaeological excavations here. The ground plans of several stone buildings were traced, together with evidence for development from shortly after the Conquest right through to the later fourth century. The buildings occupied relatively spacious plots, and were associated with larger enclosed paddocks or fields, in which there were traces of timber buildings such as barns and outhouses.

Once again, human burials were being made here in the third and fourth centuries, small cemeteries developing towards the back of the enclosed plots that lay behind the buildings lining the road. This appears to be a more haphazard development than the Northover cemetery, and no burials suggesting high status were found. It is possible that some of these cemeteries were specifically associated with the owners or occupiers of individual suburban properties, buried after death on their own land.

Another, smaller suburb developed along the Dorchester road to the

Excavating Roman buildings beside the Fosse Way in the southern suburbs.

A fourth-century well excavated in the southern Fosse Way suburbs.

south. This contained more road-frontage buildings of both wood and stone, set within larger bounded plots that were then later used for burial. A much more extensive suburb developed west of the town, although its remains and extent are relatively unexplored. There is evidence for at least one road heading towards the river here, stone and timber buildings, semi-industrial activities, and further burials. It has been suggested that port facilities developed along the river frontage which bounds this area, and remains can sometimes be seen exposed in the bank.

THE LATE ROMAN TOWN

By the middle of the fourth century *Lendiniae* had probably reached the height of its prosperity, with perhaps two or three thousand inhabitants. The provision of defences around the town centre provides some evidence of public works and further support for the claim of an enhanced status. The first defences were probably raised around the end of the second century, when a clay rampart up to twelve metres wide was constructed, using material excavated from a broad but fairly shallow ditch that ran contiguously outside the bank. The ramparts enclosed approximately ten hectares of the town centre, burying the remains of some earlier buildings. There may have been up to five gates through the defences, located on the major roads from the town. Only the Dorchester Gate has been partly excavated, where a semi-circular stone tower foundation survived on the west side of the road. There will have been similar gates on the Fosse Way – by the river crossing and to the south-west – while minor roads probably ran via by gates to the east and west. Within less than a century parts of this earthwork boundary had been built over and partly erased, and thus we can no longer discover its full height or other details of its construction.

Many towns in Britain built defences of this type at around the turn of the second and third centuries, and there have been suggestions of a link with the political upheavals of that time, when one of Britain's governors (Clodius Albinus) attempted to make himself emperor. In reality, the evidence, as here at Ilchester, is rarely precise enough to support such a claim, and some town defences were certainly built earlier. The defences are as likely to reflect a wish to express the prestige and status of a town by its chief citizens, although apart from the gates, they were soon abandoned.

Towards the end of the third century and through much of the fourth there was a more widespread and determined effort to build and maintain defences around many British towns. Once again, fashion or official status may have been a factor, but later in the fourth century, in times of increasing political instability, many were doubtless glad of their walls. At Ilchester, excavations have shown that a solidly constructed stone wall was set into the front of the old clay rampart, possibly in the AD 320s, although its dating is still uncertain. None of this wall survives above ground today, mainly because Ilchester was surrounded by a new town wall in the thirteenth century, whose builders almost certainly used the Roman wall as a quarry. Some towns still have substantial portions of their walls surviving, from which we might estimate that Ilchester's walls stood four or five metres high. The original gates will also have been maintained, although it is not known whether they were rebuilt.

Like the clay bank and ditch, Ilchester's stone wall only enclosed about 10 hectares of the town centre, and the almost filled-in ditch does not seem to have been re-dug. Outside the walls the road and riverside suburbs appear to have continued to flourish, indeed the fourth century looks to have been the period of their greatest prosperity and expansion. However, by the last decades of the century some of the suburbs may have been in decline, although burials were still being made at Northover, seemingly into the early years of the fifth century. Within the walls also, life almost certainly continued for a while into the fifth century, but whatever its ultimate fate Ilchester gradually stopped functioning as a town in the way that it had for the previous 350 years of Roman administration.

SIX

The Smaller Towns

In Britain today, the great majority of us live in towns and cities, but the Romans found none that they could clearly recognise at the time of the Conquest. The town or city-state was a key element in Roman society, and the foundation and fostering of towns as an instrument of both local and imperial government within a newly annexed territory was fundamental to the success of its integration into the Empire. This was initially achieved through the *civitas* capitals, or county towns, set up as centres for the newly established, tribal-based districts (*civitates*).

Although Somerset was divided between three *civitates*; that of the Dumnonii to the west, the Durotriges in the centre, and the Dobunni to the north, none of their capitals lie within the present county. However, the two most important towns – Bath and Ilchester – may subsequently have assumed some of the functions of what we would now think of as county towns. Both were located within particularly prosperous regions, with notable concentrations of wealthy landowners in the surrounding countryside, and probably lay at the centres of distinct pre-Roman tribal territories. These sub-divisions within the larger tribal groups continued to be recognised within the Roman system of local government, and were known as *pagi*, from which the word 'pagan' derives – people of the country.

This historical status will have been an important stimulus to the initial development of Bath and Ilchester, but can it be recognised anywhere else in Somerset? Urban development depended upon more than administrative status. As is still the case today, a town's prosperity is largely based upon trade, industry, and its role as a provider of services to its local community. Most of the other settlements in Somerset that might be called towns appear to be much smaller than Bath or Ilchester, and we know relatively little of their character or extent, let alone their status. The one exception to this is Fosse Lane, near Shepton Mallet, where a series of recent excavations and surveys have given us a vivid picture of life within a small roadside town.

SHEPTON MALLET

As its name suggests, the Fosse Lane settlement lies on the Fosse Way, just east of Shepton Mallet, and a little over halfway between Bath and

An aerial view of excavations taking place in the Roman town at Shepton Mallet; the Fosse Way is clearly marked by the modern Fosse Lane (left).

Ilchester. The site was first discovered in the nineteenth century, when the Somerset and Dorset Railway cut across it and a large Roman building was found. However, it was not until the 1990s that a series of developments prompted archaeological excavations and surveys, which led to an awareness of its true importance.

A small Iron Age farm was established here before the Romans arrived, and there may have been a fort somewhere nearby. The army was active in the area soon after the Conquest, supervising the lead and silver mines on Mendip. Apart from building the Fosse Way, they were probably also responsible for the main access road to the mines along the top of the hills, which crosses the Fosse Way at Beacon Hill, a mile or two to the north. It might be wondered why the Roman town did not develop at that junction, although even today the crossing remains very exposed. The more sheltered valley side to the south, overlooking the River Sheppey, was evidently favoured early on, and development began along the roadside during the later years of the first century.

From what has been excavated so far, it appears that a series of plots were laid out on either side of the Fosse Way, marked out by ditches and drystone wall boundaries. These are not always regular, but suggest that most buildings were initially concentrated on the road frontage, while the elongated plots behind may have been gardens, working areas or paddocks for livestock. Some buildings were later sited in these back plots, which began to be divided up as the population grew during the

The remains of a second-century stone house excavated at Fosse Lane.

second century. The settlement is built on Lias limestone, an excellent building stone, and it was not long before substantial, mortared stone buildings with stone tile roofs appeared.

At its greatest extent, the town spread for almost one kilometre along both sides of the road, and for several hundred metres back from the frontage to the east. Most of our knowledge of the settlement so far has come from these backyard areas, which suggest that it was never densely built-up. Little of the road frontage has yet been excavated, where shops, houses and perhaps a few public buildings will have been set more closely together.

Several gravelled streets served the back plots, and as time went on the number of buildings there increased. Not all were of stone, and no mosaic pavements or underfloor heating systems have yet been found, although some of the grander buildings had painted walls and glass windows. These were presumably dwellings, where extended families and perhaps slaves and servants lived, although houses could also double as workshops and as shops when alongside the main road. There is some evidence for metalworking (iron and lead), and for several kilns and ovens on the site, although many activities left few easily identifiable traces.

Animal remains suggest that sheep, goats and cattle were driven in from farms in the surrounding countryside, rather than being bred in the settlement itself. Some will have been marketed live, while others

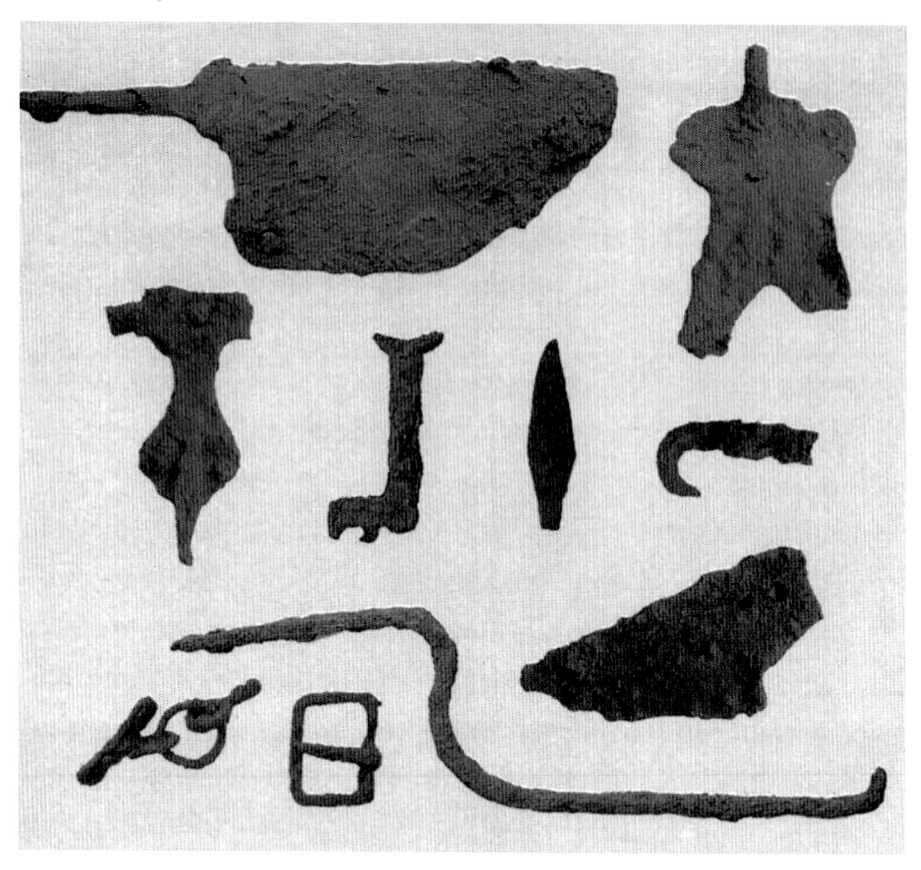

Iron objects found at Fosse Lane (top left to bottom right): cleaver, ox shoe, bucket mount, key, spearhead, pruning hook, chain links, buckle, latch lifter, ploughshare.

provided meat, milk and dairy produce, skins (leather and wool), as well as sources of bone and horn. Some of the plots and paddocks were probably for penning livestock before slaughter or sale. There is evidence for crops such as wheat, barley and oats being stored here, as well as the querns and millstones for producing flour. There were ovens for drying crops or malting grain for brewing, and probably for baking bread.

Daily life is illustrated by a whole range of tools, implements, jewellery and other personal items. Iron axes, knives, chisels, awls and cleavers were used in such trades as wood, stone or leatherworking, thatching, butchery and related occupations. The people at Fosse Lane wore rings and bracelets, bronze and bone pins in their hair, and brooches, pins and buckles on their clothes, although the clothes themselves do not survive. Some of them carried keys, nail cleaners and other toilet instruments, *styli* for writing on wax, and of course coins, many of which must have been dropped and lost in dusty or muddy streets, or beneath wooden floors.

Pottery was used widely for storing and cooking food, as well as for tableware: more rarely, glass and metal vessels of bronze or pewter have also been found. Some of the pottery was made locally, and fired in the kilns further down the valley to the west of the town, but a large proportion was imported, especially black burnished ware from Poole Harbour, finer table-wares from Oxfordshire and the New Forest, and Samian ware from Gaul. A rarer import was wine or oil, brought in large amphorae originating mostly from Spain.

No public buildings have yet been identified in the Fosse Lane settlement, although it probably boasted one or two temples, and an official posting station (the *cursus publicus*) could have been located here on the main road to the South West, providing overnight accommodation and perhaps a change of horses. We have no Roman name for this settlement, or knowledge of its precise status, though its development could reflect a *pagi* based upon a pre-existing tribal sub-group. A minor local aristocratic family could well have owned and fostered its development, perhaps even living within the settlement or in a nearby villa.

The large Iron Age hillfort at Maesbury, on top of Mendip and overlooking the site, may be a reflection of a pre-Roman tribal identity for this region. Another factor in its development could have been its frontier location, on the margin of the *civitas* of the Dobunni (or possibly the Belgae) and close to the boundary with that of the Durotriges to the south. Whatever the status of Fosse Lane, above all it must have benefited from its position on the busy Fosse Way, as well as serving its locality, much as a small country market town does today.

By the fourth century, Fosse Lane seems to have been a flourishing settlement with a likely population of several hundred; a mixture of tenants, owner-occupiers, freed slaves, slaves and artisans, the majority of local origin but with the occasional immigrant. Life for some will have been hard, but others achieved a reasonable level of wealth, if not quite matching the style of those living in their country villas, or in Bath and Ilchester. Theirs was a prosperity shared with much of the West Country in the late Roman period, though it did not last long.

Only from the end of the fourth century can some of the citizens of Fosse Lane first be identified by their remains; as a scatter of graves across some of the plots and abandoned building sites of the town, but there should be many more from the earlier years of the settlement whose remains have yet to be found.

In many ways Fosse Lane seems to be typical of the smaller roadside settlements of Roman Britain. Further up the Fosse Way towards Bath is another, apparently rather similar settlement at Camerton. Here too was a scatter of roadside buildings, the majority of stone and of simple rectangular plan. Most of what has been excavated here relates to third and fourth century occupation, when, like Fosse Lane, the settlement seems to have been most prosperous. We know less about its full extent or layout, although a number of lanes or side streets have been found. Some more elaborate buildings lay well back from the road, including two whose plans compare with those of simple corridor villa buildings, while a third may have been a shrine or temple. The settlement apparently originated in the later first century, represented by the remains of timber buildings, before stone became more widely used.

Like Fosse Lane, there was an Iron Age settlement nearby, and finds of early military equipment suggest the proximity of a fort, although this has yet to be traced. One of the most interesting aspects of this settlement is the evidence for metalworking found in some of the buildings that lie close to the road. This included several hearths or furnaces, and two stone moulds for the casting of pewter vessels – one an oval dish and the other a skillet, or *paterae*. No pewter vessels have yet been found here, but *paterae* of this type were deposited in the sacred springs at Bath. Camerton appears to have been a rather smaller settlement than Shepton Mallet, and perhaps had a more specialised function, although pewter casting and metalworking were not the only occupations. It's known remains give more the impression of a roadside

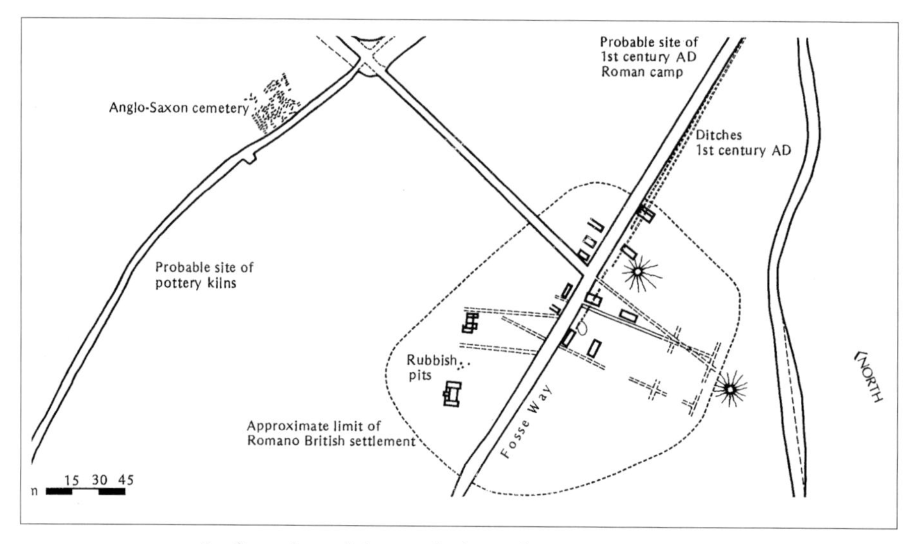

Outline plan of the roadside settlement at Camerton

An aerial view showing earthworks marking streets and plot boundaries in the mining settlement at Charterhouse on Mendip; the amphitheatre remains visible at the top, slightly left of centre.

village than a small market town. The villa-type buildings do, however, suggest the presence of wealthier members of the community, possibly its owner or an overseer. Traces of what may have been a similar settlement lie a few miles further down the road at Stratton-on-the-Fosse, close to Downside Abbey, but remain still largely unexplored.

Camerton may have owed its existence to manufacturing as much as to marketing, but an even more specialised settlement seems to have developed at Charterhouse, close to the main area of lead and silver mining on the Mendip Hills. Potentially, this is one of the most complete and best preserved Roman settlements in Somerset, surviving as low earthworks over an area of some seventeen acres in pasture fields to the north of the first-century fort. These are best seen from the air, and suggest that an irregular grid of closely-set streets separate building plots and platforms. Unfortunately, the recorded archaeological information from this site is minimal, and little else can be said of its history, layout or remains.

It was presumably lived in by those engaged in mining operations and the associated metal processing, and may also contain the remains of smelting furnaces producing lead pigs, and possibly other products such as pewter. On its south-west side are the well-preserved remains of a small amphitheatre, probably built by the army in the mid-first century but likely to have been used by the mining community thereafter. Although so little is known of the site beyond its surface remains, excavations at the nearby fort indicate that it may have been abandoned within twenty years or so, while the nearby civil settlement presumably continued to house the miners and their dependants to the end of the Roman period.

The name *Vebriacum* has been suggested for the Charterhouse settlement, or perhaps the whole imperial estate, on the basis of the first three letters –VEB – found on some of the lead pigs from the Mendip mines. An alternative name associated with this general area is *Ischalis*, from the Roman geographer Ptolemy. This name is more likely to belong to a port on the River Axe at Cheddar, at the foot of its gorge, and down which the lead from the mines could easily have been transported. What may have been a villa, and a number of other buildings representing a port or small town, have been located here close to the River Axe, which may well have been tidal up to that point.

Another small port has been identified at Crandon Bridge, near Bridgwater, on a now silted up bend of the River Parrett and at the end of the road from Ilchester along the Polden Hills. Once again, details are sparse, but discoveries made during the construction of the M5 motorway suggest that a row of rectangular stone buildings could have been warehouses within a larger settlement. A high proportion of imported pottery on the site would also support its claim as a port, where river traffic might have transhipped cargoes to sea-going vessels for export further afield.

Further downstream at Combwich are the remains of another fairly extensive riverside settlement, at an important river fording point. This could have been another small port for sea-going vessels, perhaps serving the Dumnonian communities on the west bank of the river. Too little is known of the character or extent of this settlement to speculate further, and much of it may now have been destroyed by the changing course of the river.

SEVEN

Communications & Commerce

ROADS AND RIVERS

When the Roman armies first arrived in Britain, one of their earliest tasks, once the conquest of an area was complete, was to build roads. One of the hallmarks of the Roman Empire was its road system, enabling the rapid movement of people and materials, and helping maintain its military and economic strength. Roads and trackways have existed in the landscape ever since hunters began to follow game, and especially with the establishment of agriculture and farming communities. Even before the Romans came, Britain will have been criss-crossed by a network of routes, both local and long-distance.

It is probable, though not easy to prove, that many of our existing minor roads and trackways originated in pre-Roman times. Doubtless these were used and added to in the Roman period. However, what we think of as Roman roads were usually long-distance routes, laid out in long straight stretches and carefully built by engineers and work gangs, often supervised by the army. The road surfaces were normally paved or gravelled, sometimes set on causeways or with drainage ditches alongside, and to standard widths.

Several of these roads cross Somerset, and others may yet be found. One of the earliest and most important was the Fosse Way – built in the early years of the Conquest to link the South West and the fortress at Exeter with other military bases across England as far east as Lincoln. It rapidly became one of the principal roads of Roman Britain, but almost certainly duplicates much of what had been a major prehistoric route, mainly following high ground, and which today is known as the Jurassic Way. It crossed the county from north-east to south-west, linking Bath and Ilchester via small towns at Camerton and Shepton Mallet, and continuing on to Exeter. Both Ilchester and Bath were important road junctions.

The Fosse Way at Bath was crossed by another trunk road, which started in London and ended at Sea Mills, almost on the Severn Estuary – roughly the Roman equivalent of the M4 motorway today. Ilchester was linked to the south with Dorchester, and another road ran westwards along the Polden Hills (probably also a prehistoric route) to a small town at Crandon Bridge on the estuary of the River Parrett.

The Roman road from Charterhouse on Mendip (visible as a low straight bank running diagonally across the more modern fields from bottom left to slightly right of centre top), and passing the Iron Age hillfort of Maesbury (right).

Another early cross-country route linked the Mendip lead mines with Southampton Water.

All of these roads were almost certainly laid out by the army in the first century AD, doubtless with a labour force of slaves from the tribes defeated in the early years of the Conquest. Once the region was pacified, they continued to be important for the successful development of Somerset's Roman *civitates*, who probably then maintained them until at least the fourth century – much as the County Highways Department maintains most of Somerset's roads today.

The courses of several other Roman roads have been identified, mainly in the north and east of the county, where the population was greatest. These include a road linking Gatcombe to the Avon estuary at Sea Mills, another from the Mendip lead mines northwards through the

Chew Valley to Keynsham or perhaps to Bath, and a short road which seems to link the temple on Lamyatt Beacon with the Fosse Way, south of Shepton Mallet. The long straight runs that characterise Roman roads are often a clue to their former presence, particularly when still in use today, or as tracks and boundaries. The Fosse Way is one of the best such examples, but the courses of many other roads are now obscured within the overlay of less regular routes and boundaries, or have simply been lost through disuse. The western half of Somerset is almost devoid of identifiable roads, although routes westwards along the north coast, or through the Vale of Taunton Dean, must have existed.

Many of Somerset's roads make connections with rivers, either at their crossing points, or on their estuaries. In the Roman period, and even up until the nineteenth century, waterways were a vital means of transport. Even with the vast improvement brought about by Roman road building, transportation by road was still relatively slow and costly, and wherever possible waterways would have been utilised, for bulk

A Roman milestone from Venn Bridge on the Fosse Way at Stoke-sub-Hamdon. The inscription reads: 'IMPFLVAL. SEVEROPI. OFELNOB. CAES.' 'To the Emperor Flavius Valerius Severus. Pious and fortunate, most noble Caesar' dated to AD 205-6.

cargoes in particular. Somerset's largest river, the Bristol Avon, defines much of its northern boundary, and would certainly have carried shipping upstream at least to Bath, if not beyond, from the tidal port at Sea Mills on its north bank.

The Parrett and its tributaries were perhaps the most widely used waterways, providing access well inland from its estuary and a suspected port at Crandon Bridge near Bridgwater. Ilchester, with its major road links, will have been the principal destination, via the River Yeo (or Ivel). In the previous chapter it was suggested that some straightening of its course could be attributable to the Roman period, and the growth of a port is suspected to the west of the town. Other rivers such as the Tone, the Isle, the Brue and the Axe almost certainly carried their share of traffic, as did the Congresbury Yeo in north Somerset. Today, few of these rivers are capable of carrying any significant freight, due mainly to drainage of the Levels, but there are records of medieval traffic on the Brue, the Parrett, the Tone, and the River Yeo as far as Ilchester.

Somerset's rivers all flow into the Severn Estuary, fostering such ports as Sea Mills, Crandon Bridge and perhaps also Combwich, closer to the mouth of the Parrett, and at Cheddar or Uphill on the River Axe. From these ports seagoing vessels provided links across the Bristol Channel to Wales, up the Irish Sea to Ireland and northern Britain, and southwards along the western coasts of mainland Europe and into the Mediterranean. So far, there have been no recorded discoveries of the remains of Roman ships or river craft in Somerset, unlike those found across the Severn Estuary near Caldicot in South Wales. However, such remains, preserved in the waterlogged environments of the Somerset Levels, would not be unexpected.

METALS

Perhaps the first of Somerset's minerals to be exploited were lead and silver, the latter refined from the lead. Extraction on the Mendips was underway soon after the Conquest, initially under the military supervision of the Second Legion on behalf of the emperor Claudius; mines being an imperial monopoly. The silver content of the lead is likely to have been its original attraction, as there is evidence of earlier Iron Age working at Charterhouse. This was probably the main centre, where a fort was built, the remains of which are still visible, along with what may have been a small amphitheatre. Other mining areas have been identified at Priddy, East Harptree and Green Ore.

Whatever its value as a source of silver, it was the lead itself which soon came to be valued, particularly in buildings and for the manufacture of pewter. Lead pigs, produced from the initial smelting and casting of the natural lead ore, have been found in and around the

A small, fourth-century lead pig found at Fosse Lane, Shepton Mallet, with a moulding of the producer's name – MINNIVS.

Mendip Hills, as well as from much further afield. Most of these bear inscriptions which reveal their origin and date of manufacture, from which we know that lead was being produced at least as early as AD 49. The distribution of these pigs, which were presumably lost in transit, show that most were being transported either north to the River Avon and perhaps then onwards via the port at Sea Mills, or eastwards along the road which led across Salisbury Plain to Southampton, where several pigs have been found. Mendip lead pigs have also been found in France, and had even reached Pompeii, to be made into a cistern before its burial by the eruption of Vesuvius in AD 79.

In buildings, lead was used as flashing on stone or tile roofs, for water pipes, gutters and cisterns, and as a waterproof lining, notably in the Great Bath and elsewhere in Bath. It was also used to make coffins, and for smaller items such as plugs, repair rivets or weights. Because lead is soft and melts at relatively low temperatures it can be combined with other metals, notably tin or copper. One such use with copper was the production of counterfeit coins, for which moulds of later third and fourth century type have been found on the Polden Hills.

Pewter was produced by mixing lead and tin, the tin coming from Devon and Cornwall. Some may have been produced at Charterhouse, close to the mines, but there is evidence for the production of pewter vessels at several localities in north Somerset, including the Chew Valley, Lansdown near Bath, Shepton Mallet, and at Camerton, where stone

Pewter vessels and a coin hoard with its pottery container from the peat at Shapwick, with their finder James Crane, in 1936.

moulds for casting have been found. With so much wealth focused in Bath and Ilchester, and on the country estates of local landowners, there was a considerable local market for lead as well as for pewter vessels.

After the initial period of military control the Mendip lead mines were probably leased to private producers, though still part of an imperial estate. By the time of the emperor Nero an imperial official, Gaius Nipius Ascanius, was named as controller of the lead-silver works on a lead pig made in AD 60 and found at Stockbridge in Hampshire. Later in the first century, in the reign of Vespasian, the mines were leased to a company or partnership – the *Novaec Societas* (Novaec Company), whose mark appears on two pigs from Southampton. A much smaller and more crudely made pig from Shepton Mallet has the name Minnius moulded on one side, possibly a fourth-century producer.

Iron ore can also be found in the Mendip Hills, and may have been used in small-scale smelting, but there is no evidence for significant mining or production sites, as in the nearby Forest of Dean. Iron is a relatively common mineral and various other minor sources in the rocks of Somerset could have been used, but the most significant deposits are found in the Devonian sandstones of the Brendon Hills and Exmoor. Recent research has revealed evidence of mine workings of Roman date, some of which were probably opened in the late Iron Age. Both mining and smelting sites have now been identified in the Brendon Hills. Lead, copper and silver were also mined in this part of West Somerset, although the evidence for Roman extraction is less certain.

COAL

Coal is most commonly associated with the Industrial Revolution, although it was in use as a fuel in parts of Britain from medieval times. Somerset had its own small coalfield, focused mainly upon the Radstock area south of Bath and around Nailsea, although none of the mines remain open today. The presence of coal at a number of villas and small towns or village settlements, particularly in the northern half of the county, demonstrate its Roman extraction and use. No Roman mines are known, and only surface outcrops were probably quarried; traces of which would long ago have been destroyed by later workings. Identifiable Somerset coal has been found at Camerton, Bath, the Chew Valley, at villas as far south as Lufton and Ilchester Mead, as well as at sites in Gloucestershire and Wiltshire. Despite this evidence, coal was evidently something of a curiosity, as a quote from the third-century Roman author Solinus, writing about Bath, illustrates: 'Over these springs Minerva presides and in her temple the perpetual fire never whitens to ash, but as the flame fades, turns into rocky lumps'- surely a vivid description of a coal fire?

Somerset its also rich in building stone, and a wide variety was exploited for local use, as well as for export further afield. This applied in particular to Bath stone, which was used on the more prestigious buildings of southern Britain, where its qualities as a first class freestone were much appreciated. Bath itself, and the wealthy estate owners round about, provided perhaps the largest market for the stone, which was quarried extensively on the hills overlooking the city, although much of the evidence for Roman quarries has been erased by later workings. Another high quality limestone used for building detail is found on Ham Hill, near the southern border of the county. Once again, later working has probably destroyed the original quarry sites, but the stone was used widely in villas in south Somerset and north Dorset, in particular at Ilchester, and is found at both Dorchester and Shepton Mallet.

Building in stone was widespread in Somerset from the second century onwards, and various local stone sources were quarried for this and other purposes. Perhaps the most popular was Lias limestone, a relatively common stone across large parts of central Somerset, which splits conveniently into rectangular blocks and slabs, and can also be used for paving and as roofing slate. Local sources were probably used where available, but there may have been some industrial quarrying and export, particularly of flagstone and roof slate, from the Charlton Mackrell area just north of Ilchester. Pennant sandstone was also favoured as a more durable roofing slate, outcropping in parts of north Somerset adjacent to some of the coal measures. It was used widely around the region, appearing in towns like Bath, Shepton Mallet and Ilchester, as well as on the roofs of many villas. Once again, no production site is known, but the stone can be sourced to the Radstock area.

A more specialised use of stone was for querns and millstones to grind corn, and as hones or whetstones for sharpening metal tools and weapons. Two sources have been identified in Somerset, where stone for both types of implement was both quarried and manufactured. At Pen Pits in Penselwood, on the eastern border with Wiltshire, are the pits and hollows of ancient quarry workings, where the Greensand was hard enough to make good grinding implements. Some of these workings are medieval and later, but the stone was exported widely throughout Somerset and beyond in the Roman period. A second known source was Beacon Hill, at one of the highest points of the Mendip Hills above Shepton Mallet. Here the stone was a hard, pebbly red sandstone of Devonian age, whose products are also found in Iron Age settlements such as the Glastonbury Lake Village and at Cadbury Castle. Once again, shallow pits and quarries still visibly survive, and the querns, millstones and whetstones are found at such towns as Camerton, Shepton Mallet, Ilchester, and other settlement sites.

SALT

Salt was a vital commodity in an age before the invention of refrigeration, as it was almost the only way to preserve perishable food in bulk, apart from its value as a seasoning. The north Somerset coast, with its deep, shallow estuaries and a high tidal range, was particularly suitable for salt production. The most common method was to capture the water in shallow ponds or reservoirs to settle out the silts, and then to boil it in clay pans or roughly made vessels to remove the water. In a cool and wet climate, natural evaporation by the sun was rarely feasible. Sheltered access to the sea was required, and the most favoured localities appear to have been the lower estuaries of the Rivers Parrett and Brue around Bridgwater and Highbridge. The virtual absence of production sites further up the coast is hard to explain, unless the slightly higher salinity of the water and somewhat lower silt content further west was a factor.

Many salt production sites have been recognised by the spreads of burnt clay salt boiling vessels and waste, charcoal, pottery and other debris, which often come to light when drainage ditches are dug across what is now drained pastureland. These are particularly concentrated in the Brue valley, between the Polden Hills and Wedmore, which must have been tidal marshland for much of the Roman period. The saltworkers lived on higher ground, and on what were then islands at Pawlett and Huntspill, where other salt working sites now lie buried beneath estuary silts.

Life will have been hard for these communities, particularly in the winter months, and there is little evidence of wealth here, despite the value of the salt itself. Pottery was also made in the Brue valley, partly for local use, but also perhaps to provide coarse vessels for transporting the salt for export. The saltworkers were probably employed by the owners of estates whose villas have been found on the Polden Hills and west of the River Parrett.

POTTERY

Pottery manufacture has been identified at several other sites in Somerset, but there was no major industry based in the county. Local needs were partly supplied by small-scale production, such as that linked to salt working. All were coarse wares with a relatively local distribution, whose production sources are often difficult to pinpoint. One known group of kilns was centred around Congresbury, in north Somerset, where a range of grey-ware bowls, jars and dishes were

View of a Roman pottery kiln at Shepton Mallet, as discovered in 1864, showing its interior in cross-section and some of the vessels manufactured (above).

produced, mainly for cooking and storage, and as poor-quality tableware. These supplied the local settlements, from villas and temples down to farms and villages, but their products are rarely found outside a ten-mile radius.

Another group of kilns at Shepton Mallet was firing pottery of somewhat higher quality in finer pink or orange-fired clay, which travelled rather further afield. *Mortaria* (bowls for mixing food) were one distinctive product, as were drinking tankards, and it has been suggested that the industry was set up by potters who came from the Severn Valley, possibly from around Gloucester. This was never a large manufacturing site, and later seems to have concentrated on producing coarser grey-wares for more local consumption. Larger towns like Bath and Ilchester probably also had their own locally-made wares, although kilns have yet to be found at either.

Much of Ilchester's pottery came from the potteries around Poole Harbour, whose distinctive black-burnished wares were supplied widely throughout Britain, and in particular to the army garrisons of Wales and northern Britain. Recent studies suggest that Ilchester may have been a distribution centre for this industry, located as it was on a major road to the north and to the south-west (the Fosse Way), and at the head of a navigable river with access to Wales and the north. It has been suggested that another variety of black burnished ware was made in south Somerset or north Dorset, but no manufacturing site has yet been identified.

EIGHT

The Countryside

The countryside is the product of several millennia of agricultural exploitation and development. Many of the clues to its evolution are still preserved within the landscape, and can be read - much like a document. The shape of a group of fields or their boundaries, the location of an area of woodland or common land, or the survival of earthworks on uncultivated land, can all hold keys to unlock the past. In Somerset the Romans inherited an already well developed and mature landscape, whose agricultural variety and wealth was firmly established, but to which they made their own special contribution.

THE RURAL ECONOMY

Somerset sits astride an agrarian and economic frontier in Britain, separating what is sometimes termed the Highland Zone (small, scattered settlements and a predominantly pastoral economy) and the Lowland Zone (larger settlements, including villages, and a predominantly arable economy). Needless to say, this is a very simplified if valid model, which helps to distinguish the rural (Highland Zone) economy of west Somerset from the remainder (Lowland Zone). A more appropriate terminology might be 'native landscape' and 'villa landscape' economies, both of which are certainly recognisable in Roman Somerset, and to some extent the distinction survives to this day.

At the time of the Roman Conquest Iron Age society was based upon tribal units dominated by kin-based elites, whose wealth derived from agricultural surpluses. Most of the people lived in individual family farm units, whether as freemen and their families or as slaves. Larger groups sometimes lived within hillforts, or more open settlements, particularly in the South East. Annexation by Rome brought a new government to southern Britain, but much of the native agricultural system and local political hierarchy remained, adapting to and integrating with the new organisation and its obligations.

In Somerset some new landowners will have appeared, including absentee landlords from outside. Some land would have been directly owned by the emperor, as for example the Mendip lead and silver mines, which could well have been part of a much larger imperial agricultural estate. However, unlike the Norman Conquest, when virtually all the

A general view of the mosaic pavement from the villa at Low Ham, depicting scenes from Virgil's *Aeneid*.

Saxon landlords were displaced, the majority of the native British aristocracy remained, to form the governments of the new *civitates*, and as time went on, as residents on their country estates.

VILLAS AND ESTATES

In many ways the Roman villa epitomises our idea of the Romans and their way of life. Villas were among the earliest sites to be explored archaeologically in Britain in the eighteenth and early nineteenth centuries; the discovery of mosaic pavements, painted walls, heated bathhouses and suites of rooms, capturing the imagination of the educated public. In reality these establishments were very much the exception, but nevertheless they do reflect the highest aspirations of contemporary classical culture, and they do set the standards to which the most wealthy and influential members of Romano-British society would have aspired.

Somerset has one of the greatest known concentrations of villas in Britain, some of which were grand houses, although many did not fully develop until the last century or so of the Roman administration. The towns of Bath and Ilchester were the focus for notable groups; there are twenty or more within five miles of Bath and over thirty within ten miles of Ilchester. Despite their high profile, relatively few have been extensively or well excavated. Where we have sufficiently detailed information it is clear that there was considerable variation in the scale and status of different establishments, and thus no doubt between their owners.

The largest and most sophisticated were often built around large courtyards or gardens; the main house including elaborate mosaic pavements, painted walls and ceilings, special dining or reception rooms, separate bath suites, underfloor heating, and colonnaded verandas or decorative facades. Some of the grandest have been found around Bath, as at Keynsham, Newton St Loe, Wellow, and further south at Holcombe; or the neighbouring villas at Pitney and Low Ham, not far from Ilchester. Both Keynsham and Holcombe had elaborate dining rooms, and another villa at Lufton, near Yeovil, had an extraordinary octagonal room containing a plunge bath attached to the main building.

Decorative mosaic floors are a notable feature of the main residential rooms in many of these villas, featuring elaborate patterned or figured designs. Scenes from classical literature or religion were popular themes, perhaps the finest and best preserved mosaic from Somerset being the pavement from Low Ham featuring scenes from Virgil's *Aeneid*. Newton St Looe featured an Orpheus pavement, and the villa at Whatley, near Frome, may have had another, as well as a representation of the goddess

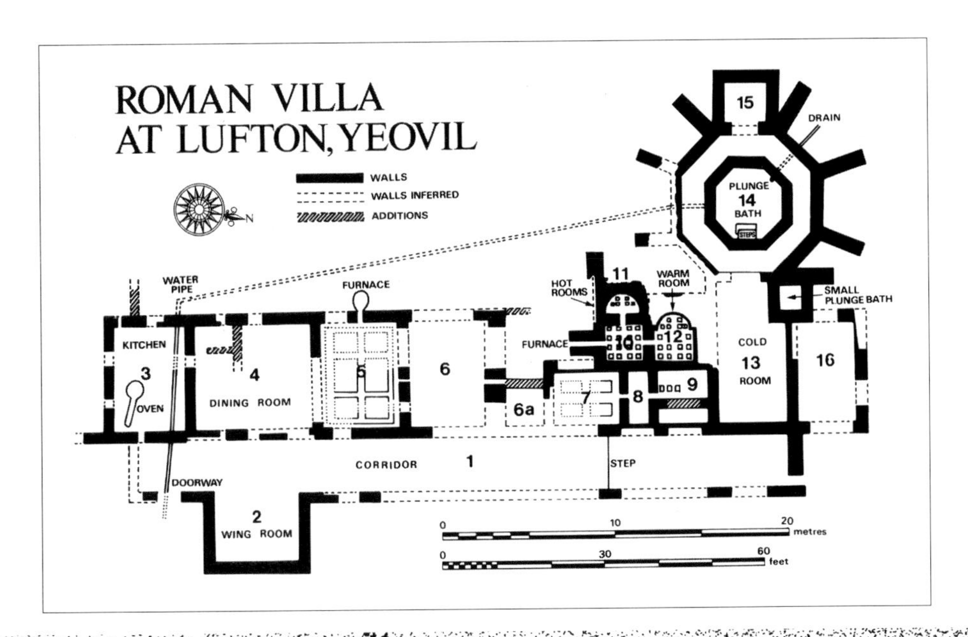

Lufton Roman villa, a plan and reconstruction view of the main house.

Cybele. Another exceptional mosaic was the Four Season's pavement from Pitney, and the fragment of a hunting scene from East Coker may come from another. What may have been an exceptional villa at Gatcombe, south of Bristol, appears to have been destroyed by the railway in the nineteenth century, but was distinguished by the building

'The Four Seasons' mosaic pavement from Pitney Roman villa.

of a massive defensive stone wall around it in the fourth century. At Westland, in the suburbs of Yeovil, another large villa ranged around a courtyard was built adjacent to an extensive area of settlement. This lay beside the road from Ilchester to Dorchester, and might have been another small roadside town.

The settlement at Westland is a reminder that villas were not the isolated country houses that their remains sometimes suggest. At Pitney, where several ranges of buildings were grouped around a large courtyard, an attempt has been made to identify a variety of functions, from barns, animal sheds and processing areas, to residential quarters for the estate workers as well as the owner and his family. This interpretation is based primarily upon the layout of the buildings, and has been attempted at other sites. Some villas appear to have more than one principal dwelling house, and it has been suggested that two (or more) families may have shared one estate; possibly a reflection of

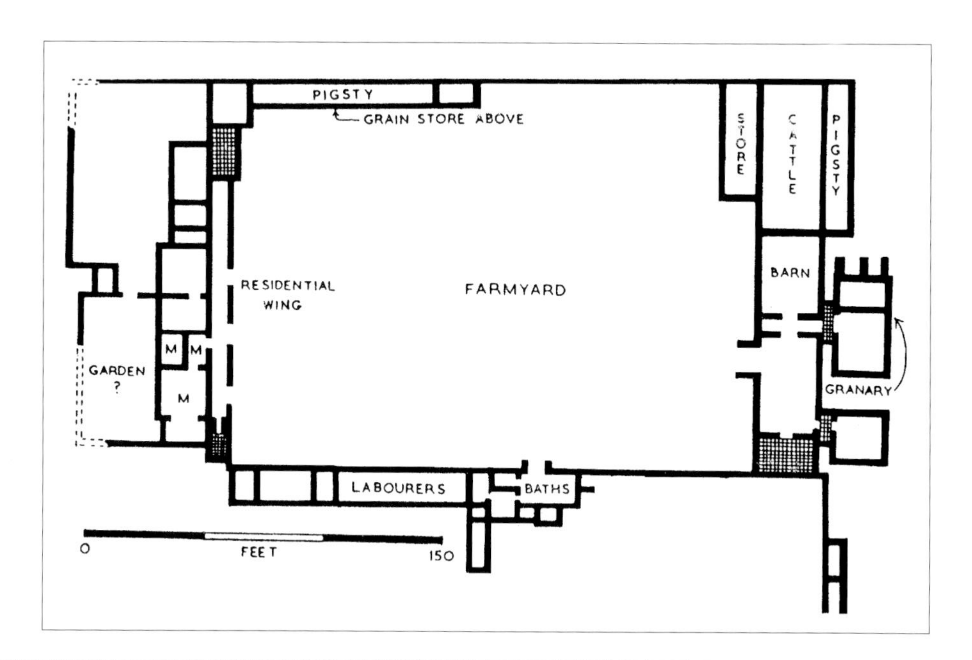

A plan of the main buildings at Pitney Roman villa and a reconstruction of what they may once have possibly looked like.

divided or partiable inheritance from pre-Roman times. The villa at Halstock, south of Yeovil and just in Dorset, is a potential example.

Primary evidence for the agricultural basis of these estates, in the form of crop or animal remains and their products, is harder to come by. When found, the carbonised remains of crops demonstrate that spelt wheat was the most commonly grown grain, along with some oats, barley and rye. The quantities of animal bones found give the impression that cattle were extensively farmed, a trend that seems to have intensified as time went on. Pigs, horses, sheep and goats were also kept in lesser numbers, although as today, some farms will have specialised. At Pitney, for example, pig rearing has been suggested, while on a smaller nearby farm site at Bradley Hill, sheep were predominant. In the same area, the farm settlement at Catsgore and the villa at Ilchester Mead concentrated on cattle, although other animals were kept and crops were also grown and processed at both sites. All of these estates are quite close to Ilchester, where animals will have been driven to market, or where their products like wool, leather, or horn were processed and sold. This is backed up by the character of the crop and animal remains analysed from towns like Ilchester and Shepton Mallet, as well as the discovery of small plots and paddocks for penning animals in transit.

We may never have enough information to reconstruct a detailed portrait of Somerset's farming regime in the Roman period, but it is clear from studies here and elsewhere in Britain that cattle became progressively more popular and that improved breeding produced larger and longer-lived animals. This trend probably reflects Roman tastes, and the long-term demands of the army and the growing urban population within the province of Britain. Parts of Somerset remain to this day well-known for their dairy cattle, and there is little doubt that the later Roman prosperity of so many villa estates owed much to livestock rearing. However, unlike today, the farming on most estates will have been mixed, with a much higher degree of self-sufficiency. Some, indeed, may have been engaged in other commercial activities. The villas at Combe Down, Bath and Bedmore Barn inside Ham Hill may have operated stone quarries, while a small villa at Chew Park was apparently involved in metalworking connected with the Mendip mining industry. The Chew Park villa is a good example of the more modest establishments that are found widely in Britain and throughout the Empire. These most typical building types are classified as winged corridor villas, and two others lie adjacent to the roadside settlement at Camerton.

Villas represent the top of the social ladder, in the countryside at least, although the definition of what constitutes a villa in Britain is not always so clear cut as there was considerable variation in the styles of building and their level of sophistication. This is certainly the case in Somerset, where the majority of villa owners were probably prosperous local landowners – the descendants of the native aristocracy – rather than great magnates. Whatever their status, their prosperity was dependent upon the labour of others, relatively few of whom will have been resident at the villa itself. Our understanding of the Romano-British countryside has long been dominated by villas and their remains, but as detailed local studies now demonstrate, villas are but one element within a well-populated rural society.

Unlike today, farming was labour-intensive, employing the great majority of the Romano-British population, as it did in Britain until the Industrial Revolution. Studies carried out in Somerset, and elsewhere, have shown that settlements are commonly distributed well within a kilometre of each other on average, particularly in the wealthiest areas. Perhaps the best excavated site in Somerset is the village at Catsgore, where a group of stone farmhouses and other structures clustered alongside the road from Ilchester to the port at Crandon Bridge. At least seven separate properties can be identified within individual plots; some founded in the second century, but close to the site of an earlier Iron Age settlement. Based on a mixed agricultural economy, though where cattle seem to have been dominant, the village prospered until well into the fourth century. It has been suggested that the village was lived in by tenant farmers, and that what may have been its parent villa lay slightly to the south-west.

The buildings excavated at Gatcome in north Somerset could have been part of another village settlement, though perhaps more intimately associated with a villa estate, as may have been the Westland settlement. Sometimes the relationship between village-type settlements and a villa estate is less obvious, as is the case with the mainly second and third–century village at Heriots Bridge in the Chew Valley, although even where no nearby villa is known the dependency of such sites upon a landlord must be suspected.

To the east of Ilchester a sprawling settlement of scattered buildings, enclosures and lanes has been identified by aerial photography between Yeovilton and Podimore, where some excavation has recently taken place. This was evidently preceded by a nearby Iron Age settlement, and appears to be one of several along the valley of the River Yeo – a further testament to the prosperity of Ilchester and its surroundings.

Aerial view of cropmarks showing field boundaries, droveways and settlement plots on the site of the Romano-British village at Podimore, near Ilchester.

A little further to the east, intensive field surveys centred upon the hillfort of Cadbury Castle are revealing more village-type settlements. One of these occupied the valley alongside the hillfort to the east and immediately adjacent to the medieval settlement of South Cadbury. A second lies on hills to the south-east of Cadbury, at Sigwells, where geophysical surveys, fieldwalking and some excavation have taken place. Here, a scatter of stone and timber buildings lie within a series of small fields and paddocks, and there is evidence for some re-planning of its layout in the later Roman period, as well as a long history of prehistoric land use. At least one other smaller farm site lies closer to the hillfort, also within a small set of enclosures, and others are suspected in the locality. There is a notable gap in the distribution of villas in this area to the east of Ilchester, which may signify a larger than average rural estate, perhaps connected directly with Ilchester itself or a major absentee landlord such as the emperor.

Another area where intensive fieldwork has recently been undertaken is around the village of Shapwick, on the north slope of the Polden Hills. Fieldwalking, supported by some geophysical surveys and excavation sampling, has revealed at least nine separate settlements within the parish. Two of these can be identified as villas; one later becoming the site of the early medieval church and manor house, while the other produced a remarkable hoard of silver coins. These were apparently concealed early in the third century beneath the floor of one room, and constitute the largest recorded hoard of Roman silver coins ever found in Britain (9,733 denarii). This is not the first hoard to have been found at Shapwick, or at other sites along the Polden Hills, and the Poldens may have been a particularly wealthy area in the later Roman period. The Shapwick survey has also demonstrated the close relationship between Romano-British and earlier Iron Age settlements; a pattern which recurs again and again in Somerset, and reminds us of its rich prehistoric agricultural inheritance.

Before the Roman Conquest individual farmsteads were the backbone of Iron Age tribal society and its economy. Most of the best-known examples have been found in the northern part of the county, including Chew Park, Butcombe, Camerton and Cannards Grave, some of which were occupied into the Roman period. These were open settlements, often containing timber roundhouse dwellings and other buildings for storage, processing and penning animals, and may have housed extended families. Where information is available, sheep and goats were more common than cattle, although grain and other crops were also cultivated. These were the basic working farm units of the late prehistoric agricultural system, and initially, life within them was little changed by the coming of Rome.

Their Romano-British heirs soon began to adopt some of the new fashions in domestic and working equipment, and numerous farms and

Some of the 9,733 silver denarii from a villa at Shapwick, the largest hoard of Roman silver coins ever found in Britain.

small settlement sites are recognised throughout the county today by surface scatters of coins, pottery and other artefacts. Building designs and agricultural operations within these farms were slower to change. Circular buildings were still in use at Catsgore, for example, in the third century, and while rectangular building plans were increasingly adopted, mortared stone buildings will always have been the exception. Few sites have been explored sufficiently to gain a clear picture of their typical characteristics. One exception is the farm at Bradley Hill, on the limestone hills just north of Ilchester. Here, two stone houses and a barn were built in the fourth century, close to the site of an earlier late Iron Age farm. From the quantity and character of animal bones found, this was evidently a sheep farm, whose fourth and fifth-century inhabitants were also being buried in a small cemetery alongside. Houses of similar size and layout have been found at Sigwells, near South Cadbury, where sheep and wool production may also have been pre-eminent.

Much of Somerset lay within the lowland zone of Britain, where what can be termed a villa-based economy operated. To the west, a different picture emerges, where the impact of Rome was less and the pattern of farming and settlement continued much as it had during the Iron Age. The South West peninsula of Britain, of which West Somerset is a part, is regarded as belonging to the highland or native landscape zone; a distinction which seems to be further emphasised by a political boundary – along the River Parrett – between the Durotriges to the east and the Dumnonii to the west.

In this region villas are few and far between, and the character of the bulk of rural settlements is also different. Aerial photography has revealed numerous ditched enclosures in the Vale of Taunton Deane and along the fringes of the Quantock and Brendon Hills. Most of these are still undated, but many are probably the sites of Iron Age and Romano-British farms; like the small circular or rectangular enclosures which characterise numerous contemporary farms in western Britain. Many settlement sites can, nevertheless, be identified by finds, as is the case for the rectangular ditched enclosure at Maidenbrook Farm, on the outskirts of Taunton. This succeeded an Iron Age settlement, and in the second century both circular and rectangular buildings were contained within the compound, to be superseded later by larger plots or paddocks defined by slighter boundary ditches and drystone walls. Part of another later settlement of similar character exists at Holway, in the southern suburbs of Taunton. These sites were relatively Romanised, particularly by the third and fourth centuries, and it is possible that more villas may yet be discovered in the Taunton Deane area.

Little is known of the economy of these settlements, although mixed agriculture featuring both livestock and arable farming is likely in the more fertile lowland areas. Further west, the uplands of the Brendon Hills and Exmoor would have been suitable for sheep, where the small individual farms probably changed little from those of the Iron Age. No villages or towns have been identified in the area, although its inhabitants were no less part of the civil province of Britain; adopting Roman fashions in pottery, jewellery, tools and furnishings, and paying their taxes like everyone else, whether in coin, or perhaps more often in kind.

NEW LANDS

The Polden Hills and their extension to the north of Ilchester overlook the Somerset Levels, and one factor in the prosperity of this region may have been the exploitation of the Levels. At the time of the Roman conquest the Somerset Levels, north and south of Mendip, were largely undrained wetlands. Such areas were by no means wastes. The dryer parts provided rich summer grazing as well as winter fodder. Peat was cut for fuel, salt was produced on the tidal margins, and there was an abundance of fish and wildfowl. It has been suggested that the southern levels were effectively a frontier region in the Iron Age, and that the Lake Villages of Glastonbury and Meare were neutral ground; centres for social and commercial exchange. Even after the arrival of the Romans, this area was divided between the three *civitates* of the Dobunni, Durotriges and Dumnonii, but it was not long before the agricultural potential of the Levels was realised by its new landlords.

In eastern England the Fens were settled and drained from towards the end of the first century, largely perhaps under the aegis of an imperial estate. On the Welsh side of the Severn Estuary, reclamation may also have been a state initiative, linked with the legionary garrison at Caerleon. In Somerset the timing and pattern of reclamation appears to be rather different. Private enterprise seems to have been the prime factor, with settlement and exploitation widespread by the third and fourth centuries, although the reclamation process probably began earlier. This is the period of maximum prosperity in the Roman West Country, and it is surely no coincidence that the Somerset Levels, north and south of Mendip, are surrounded by numerous villa-based estates.

Drainage and land reclamation has two somewhat contradictory requirements. On the one hand the sea must be excluded, while on the other excess fresh water must be able to run off. In the late Iron Age and early Roman period there is evidence for a slightly warmer climate, and a halt or even slight drop in the general sea level rise that had been underway since the end of the last Ice Age. Even the most modest changes will have been advantageous. Another ally were the sand dune formations along much of the southern coast of the Severn Estuary, which effectively acted as a sea wall. The only exception is the section of coast between Clevedon and Middle Hope, north of Weston-super-Mare, where an artificial sea bank must have been constructed.

Sea banks would also have been required along the tidal river estuaries; namely the north bank of the Brue, and both banks of the Axe and the Congresbury Yeo. The major exception was the Parrett and lower Brue valley, which seem to have remained an area of undrained saltmarsh that turns to freshwater peat moor further inland. This must have been a deliberate strategy, since salt production is concentrated in this region throughout most of the Roman period, while the moors were doubtless being exploited for their peat, fishing and game. The creation and maintenance of these reclamation works required huge resources; though whether by central authority or private enterprise is unclear.

Once land had been drained and reclaimed, it was quickly settled and used for both arable and grazing. There are several examples in north Somerset, notably around the villages of Congresbury and Yatton, where there was a villa, pottery kilns, farms and village settlements; as well as the temple at Henley Wood and the Iron Age hillfort at Cadbury, reoccupied in the late fifth century. Nearby was another villa at Wemberham, built on the drained moors close to the River Yeo, and further north the walled villa estate of Gatcombe. Much of this reclaimed land is now unploughed pasture, and remarkably, some remains of the settlements and their fields still survive as earthworks on the Congresbury Moors. Similar evidence survives on the adjacent Banwell Moors to the west, where another large villa stood on the moor edge, with others nearby at Winthill and at Locking.

On the south side of the Mendip Hills there is earthwork evidence for fields and settlements on the drained levels of the Axe Valley north of Wedmore, and well-preserved field systems on the lower slopes of the hills further west around Bleadon. Such remains are obscured further south by post-Roman flood alluvium, but seem to be just as extensive. The 'island' of Brent, with its hillfort and possible temple site, was probably the principal focus of this area, and the location of another villa estate centre at Lakehouse Farm.

The wealth and importance of the Polden Hills in the later Roman period has already been mentioned. A series of villas can be identified along the Hills, from Crandon Bridge and Woolavington, to Cossington and Shapwick. There is less evidence for new drainage of land here, but these villas may well have profited from the salt industry in the Brue Valley. Finally, the concentration of wealthy estates to the north of Ilchester surely owed their prosperity in part to the exploitation of the adjacent levels south of the Polden Hills. The villas at Pitney and Low Ham are among the richest of late Roman Britain, and there are half a dozen more nearby in the Somerton and Compton Dundon area.

NINE

The Spiritual Realm

Religion and ritual played a much larger part in the lives of our ancestors than it does for the majority today. Before the coming of Christianity to Roman Britain, its inhabitants embraced a variety of spiritual beliefs, many of which are inaccessible to us now. The native inhabitants were undoubtedly in much closer touch with the spirit of the earth, as expressed in its seasons and elements, natural phenomena, special places, and the movements of the sun, moon, stars and planets. Such beliefs and concerns can motivate a variety of responses, some of which are recorded by classical writers, while traces of others may be detected in the archaeological record. Rome had its own set of beliefs centred on gods and goddesses like Jupiter, Mars, Mercury, Aphrodite, or Minerva, and readily embraced those of its neighbours or conquered territories. In Britain, and elsewhere within the Celtic realms of Europe, elements of the native religion were absorbed, although native deities were frequently romanised through association with the classical gods and goddesses – Sul Minerva at Bath is a classic instance.

SHRINES AND TEMPLES

Iron Age centres for ritual or religious observance are difficult to identify from surviving remains, although many sites may be suspected. Rivers and their sources in wells and springs were revered, and the presence of burials and other finds close to the notable risings at Wells and Wookey Hole, suggests that this continued into the Roman period. Elsewhere, this prehistoric uncertainty is transformed by the appearance of distinctive buildings, or the expression of beliefs or deities that survive in stone and metal inscriptions or images. Somerset has an exceptional number of sites where the remains tell us much about the character of religion and worship in Roman Britain.

One of the earliest lay within the ramparts of Cadbury Castle, where the rectangular foundations of a small timber-built shrine have been excavated. We have no idea of the rituals or deities worshipped here, but there was a series of animal burials nearby, in particular of calves. The shrine was probably built soon after the storming and capture of the hillfort at the time of the Claudian invasion, but may not have outlasted a second assault on the hill and its temporary occupation by the army,

A vertical view of foundation trenches and burial pits marking the shrine excavated at Cadbury Castle.

possibly following the revolt of Queen Boudicca. Similar shrines appear elsewhere in Britain in the first century, as at Uley in the Gloucestershire Cotswolds, or on Maiden Castle in Dorset. Both of these were later developed as Romano-Celtic temples. Another may have been built later on Cadbury Hill, although its remains have not been positively identified.

Prominent hilltops were favoured sites for shrines and temples in the Roman period, and Somerset has many. Such places may well have featured in pre-Roman religion, although firm evidence is hard to come by. One group of people associated with late Iron Age ritual and religion and recorded by classical writers, notably Julius Caesar, were the druids. Druids seem to have been a powerful priesthood in Celtic society, whose influence played a major role in encouraging British resistance to the Roman Conquest in the first century. They represented aspects of native religion that Rome would not tolerate, and it is conceivable that Cadbury was a place where druids were active. Another might have been the Glastonbury 'island', with its continuing associations of spiritual power, myth and legend, and it could be significant that no later Romano-Celtic temple has so far been found at such a prominent and numinous spot.

On a clear day the summit of Cadbury Hill provides a panoramic view over much of Somerset, from Mendip to the Blackdown and Quantock Hills, and round to the coast. The sites of several Romano-Celtic temples are also visible from here, the closest on the prominent summit of Lamyatt Beacon on Creech Hill, overlooking Bruton. Excavations here in the early 1970s revealed what could be described as a classic Roman-Celtic temple plan. Typically, such temples were shrines or sanctuaries presided over by priests, where supplicants might come to make requests and bring offerings, but they were not the focus for group worship, like a Christian church or Islamic mosque. This is illustrated by the plan of the temple, which was essentially a central roofed shrine known as a *cella*, probably of two stories and surrounded by a roofed, single-storey corridor or ambulatory. The *cella* was the shrine or home of the deity, perhaps represented by a cult statue, while the ambulatories may have contained altars, other statues, and probably offerings brought by supplicants. Additional shrines flanked the main entrance

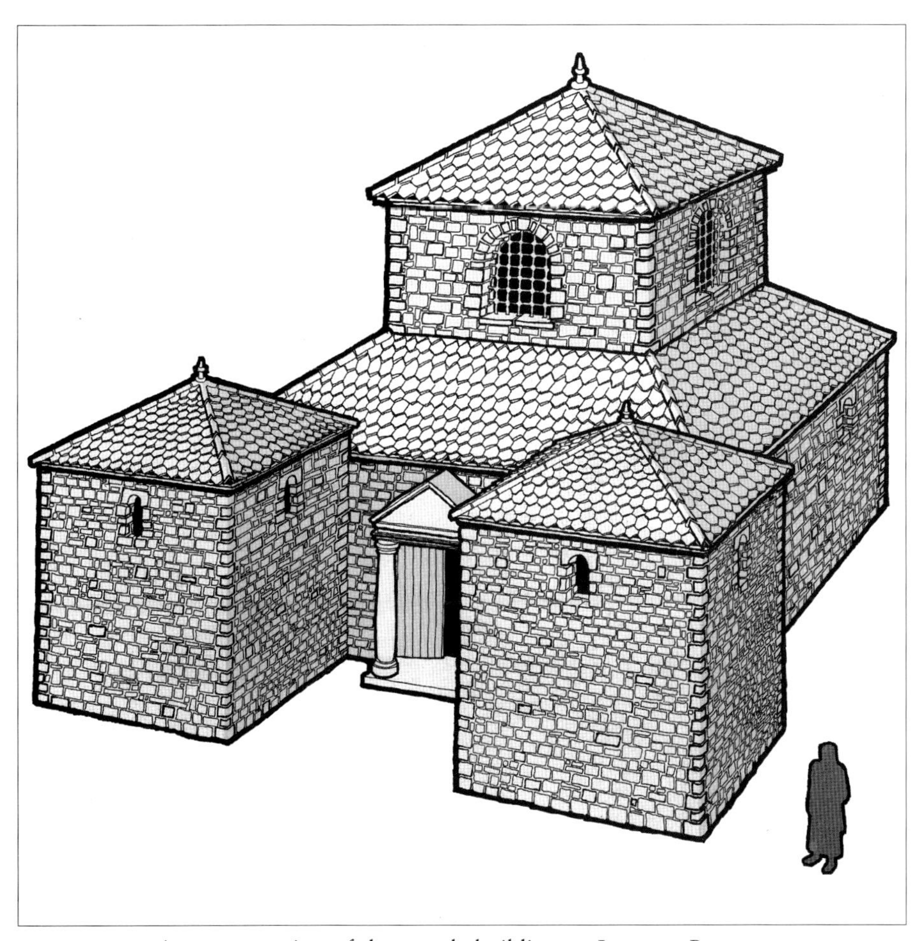

A reconstruction of the temple building on Lamyatt Beacon.

Bronze figurines from the temple on Lamyatt Beacon, depicting Roman gods – from left to right - Mercury (2), Hercules, Minerva and Mars.

and may have been dedicated to other deities. The principal deity at Lamyatt seems to have been Mars, although others such as Mercury, Jupiter, Minerva and Hercules are represented in a fine series of bronze figurines. These figures may have been dedications left by supplicants or patrons of the temple, as were the many hundreds of coins found here, and other items such as jewellery or miniature pottery vessels to hold offerings.

At the western extremity of the Mendip Hills was another temple of a similar plan, overlooking the Bristol Channel on Brean Down. This seems to have been built in the fourth century, but lies close to an earlier Bronze Age burial mound and a small Iron Age hillfort. The principal deity is unknown, but multiple dedications were common at such temples, and there may well have been an association with an original Celtic god or goddess. Both Brean Down and Lamyatt Beacon were flourishing in the fourth century, when Roman Somerset was at its most prosperous. Both are close to earlier Iron Age hillforts. Another temple not far from Brean Down is suspected on the summit of Brent Knoll, within the ramparts of the hillfort. In North Somerset more temples may have been built within hillforts; at Worlebury overlooking Weston-super-Mare, at Dolebury further east, and at Cadbury Tickenham near Clevedon.

Another North Somerset temple at Henley Wood was built adjacent to the hillfort of Cadbury Congresbury. Here, the evidence for a site with sacred associations going back to prehistoric times is stronger, as

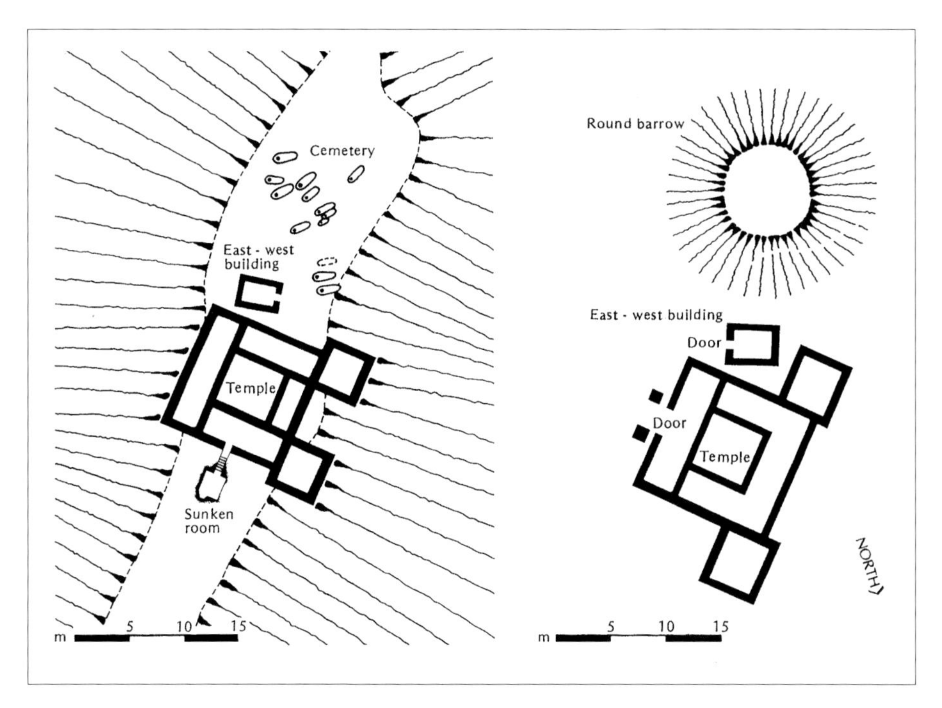

Plans of two late Roman hilltop temples in Somerset;
Lamyatt Beacon (left) and Brean Down (right).

suggested by the Celtic style of a striking little bronze female figure found there. A sequence of temple buildings can be traced, although the earliest to be clearly defined was a two-celled structure containing a massive stone base, which may have supported a cult statue or altar. This was in use during the third century, but by the fourth century the temple had been rebuilt in the classic Romano-Celtic style, with a square central *cella* surrounded by an ambulatory. Once again, we are ignorant of the deities that may have been worshipped here, but the numerous coins and finds of jewellery and other personal items could well have been left as offerings.

All of these temples appear to have stood in relative isolation on their hilltops, with perhaps one or two ancillary buildings, but another temple site in North Somerset, at Pagans Hill, Chew Stoke, was more elaborate. The Romano-Celtic style of central *cella* with an outer ambulatory was employed, but here an octagonal temple with external buttresses was built towards the end of the third century, suggesting that the whole building may have stood at least two stories high. The remains of a base to support the cult statue or altars survived within the *cella*. A stone-lined well, over 17 metres deep, lay to the west, and two ranges of stone buildings enclosed the temple precinct to the north and east. These may have provided accommodation for visitors, as well as resident priests

and other officials, and there may have been stalls here selling offerings to leave in the temple.

The association of these relatively isolated hilltop temples with prehistoric sites, especially hillforts, may be a reflection of their pre-Roman importance within Iron Age society, and indeed perhaps of the social and political divisions within that society. Were these places that represented the ancestral memory and identity of the native inhabitants, subsumed now within the governed province of Roman Britain and its somewhat artificial regional *civitates*, but who retained their sense of origin and belonging to much older communities?

Places like Cadbury Castle, Lamyatt Beacon, Brean Down or Cadbury Congresbury were surely of immense significance to different tribal groups within pre-Roman Somerset. To the Romans, it was just as important that such repositories or symbols of folk memory and identity be officially recognised and brought within the Roman system, as it was to encourage local self government and an appreciation of the merits of classical Roman civilisation.

As time went on these temples became more elaborate, patronised no doubt by those who identified with them locally, in particular the descendants of the native aristocracy. Some, like Lamyatt, were located close to the boundaries between different native tribes, and may have originally represented territorial markers or neutral ground. Others may have been places of periodic assembly, where celebration or social and commercial transactions were as important as religious observance – perhaps not unlike medieval fairs or even music festivals of today. Somerset appears to be particularly rich in these rural hilltop temples and there are undoubtedly others still awaiting discovery. The interiors or proximity of other major Iron Age hillforts may provide clues, both to their whereabouts and to the patchwork of pre-Roman allegiances and territorial entities within the county.

By far the grandest and most renowned religious site in Somerset was the classical temple and precinct dedicated to Sul Minerva in Bath (see chapter 4). Despite its sophistication, this was another sacred site rooted in native Celtic traditions, and even here the temple itself was soon adapted to the more traditional Romano-Celtic form of *cella* and ambulatory, albeit on a grand scale. Here are found many of the attributes of such religious centres – powerful natural phenomena (the springs), the marriage of native and Roman deities, the employment of offerings and dedications, and a focus for commerce. Trade was almost certainly a significant feature of most temple sites (associated in

Opposite page. Bronze figurine of a female Celtic deity from the temple at Henley Wood, Yatton.

Venus and cupids depicted in the central roundel of the mosaic from Low Ham villa.

particular with the god Mercury), and many were located in the towns and cities of the Empire. Bath almost certainly housed other temples, and more can be expected in places like Ilchester and Shepton Mallet, but with the exception of one unusual building at Camerton no others have yet been discovered in Somerset's Roman towns.

BELIEF AND BURIAL

Temples and shrines, and the dedications, offerings and representations of attending deities, are the most obvious expression of religion found in Roman Britain before the coming of Christianity. The physical remains left by Christianity are often more elusive, although as we shall see in the next chapter Christianity began to make an impact on Somerset in the fourth century, and was probably predominant by the fifth.

Bronze figurine of a Lar – a household deity – found in a limekiln at Castle Cary.

Spiritual beliefs probably played a significant role in daily life, although little of this will have left visible traces. Many homes will have had a small household shrine or corner where daily prayers or offerings were made. In wealthy villas rooms were sometimes set aside as shrines, while the provision of mosaic floors and painted walls featuring classical deities may have had religious connotations, although much of this was also inspired by literature like the *Aeneid*, as depicted on the Low Ham villa pavement.

A deity particularly associated with the home was the Lar, often depicted as a youth or child and usually present as a pair of such figures. One example from Somerset was found, rather oddly, within a limekiln in Castle Cary, placed there as part of some ritual that involved deliberately destroying part of the kiln after its final firing. The kiln was presumably supplying lime for a major building nearby, although none is known in the town. Alternatively there was another shrine or temple in the vicinity, possibly at the source of the River Cary, which lies only a few hundred metres away from the kiln. Another bronze statuette, of Mars, which may have been part of a household shrine, was found at the villa near East Coker. The statuette bore the inscription, 'to the god Mars Rigisamus, Iventus Sabinus pays his vow gladly, willingly and deservedly'. We may never know what the vow was, but is this the name of one of Somerset's wealthy landowners, perhaps an ex-soldier, enjoying retirement in his luxurious country house?

Death marks the moment when belief and ritual are often most powerfully expressed, and the remains of Somerset's Romano-British inhabitants are well represented in both cemeteries and as individual burials. At the time of the Roman Conquest, cremation was the usual burial rite, but it is rare to find such burials unless they were placed in a container or with other objects – usually certain possessions of the dead person. Disposal of the dead in Iron Age Britain is still something of a mystery, both cremation and inhumation burials are found, but what happened to the great majority of the population is unknown. Most people had probably adopted the Roman fashion for cremation by the end of the first century, but once again the quantity of such remains found so far represents but a tiny fraction of the population of Somerset in the first and second centuries.

No major cremation cemeteries have ever been excavated in the county, although chance discoveries sometimes suggest their whereabouts. One small group were located in three enclosures found at Ben's Bridge in the Chew Valley, associated with traces of second and third century occupation nearby. The greatest concentrations of people lived in towns like Bath and Ilchester, where some cremations have been found. One placed in a small lead casket was found beneath a boundary

Tombstone of a man from the Fosse Way cemetery in Bath

bank within the settlement at Shepton Mallet. Burial within settlements of the living was normally a proscribed activity in the Roman world, and the roadsides approaching a town would often be a focus for cemeteries, This was certainly so around Bath, cremations having been recorded along the Fosse Way to the west, and north along the London road in Walcot.

As we have seen, Bath is distinguished by a fine collection of sculpture and inscriptions from the tombs that lined the roads beyond its outer suburbs. Most of these were later re-used, notably in the fourth-century town walls, so we can rarely associate the tombstones with remains of the people commemorated. Most of these memorials were set up in the first and second centuries, but no other town or cemetery in Somerset is so rich in such remains. None are recorded at Ilchester for example, although once again there were cemeteries alongside the main roads out of the town. One humble, and rather touching mother's memorial to a child was found inscribed on a pottery flagon which probably accompanied a cremation alongside the Fosse Way there : M. VERINA VRILUCOLO PARBO COMTM: '(from) Verina for little Vrilucolus'.

In the third century fashions changed and burial gradually replaced cremation. Christianity, and the spread of other religions which emphasised resurrection and the afterlife may have been largely responsible, allowing us to find the remains of Somerset's later Roman population far more easily. Once again it is the towns that are the focus for the largest numbers of burials, and several cemeteries have been found and partly excavated.

Some of the best known are around Ilchester, where several hundred graves have been identified. In the south and south-western suburbs, plots or paddocks which lay behind buildings along the Dorchester and Fosse Way road frontages were being used for burial by the fourth century. Typically the dead were laid in relatively shallow graves, probably in shrouds and sometimes nailed wooden coffins, their alignment apparently determined by the arrangement of the plot boundaries. Bodies of men, women and children were normally in an extended position, face-up, with arms alongside or in different positions across the body. Sometimes bodies were placed face down, and very occasionally in a crouched or flexed position on their sides. Another unusual feature was the removal of the head after death and its placement elsewhere in the grave, usually near the feet.

Some people were buried with possessions such as knives, rings or bracelets. Some had a coin placed in their mouths. Others were accompanied by animal bones (a chicken, joint of meat, or a sheep's jaw), or pottery vessels that were often smashed. One man was buried with his dog, evidently an old and work-worn animal, but perhaps a faithful and loved companion who accompanied his master to the grave.

Many of these features represent the beliefs and rituals of the deceased and the ceremonies associated with their death and burial. Little of this can be reconstructed or understood by us today, and much perishable evidence must also now be lost. From the remains themselves we can tell that life was relatively hard and that average life expectancies for both sexes were in the thirties, although a significant proportion lived much longer. Women had a slightly shorter life expectancy than men, probably because the risks to health from childbearing were higher: female burials are sometimes found accompanied by their newborn (neonatal) infants. Disease and infection were difficult to combat, and infant mortality in

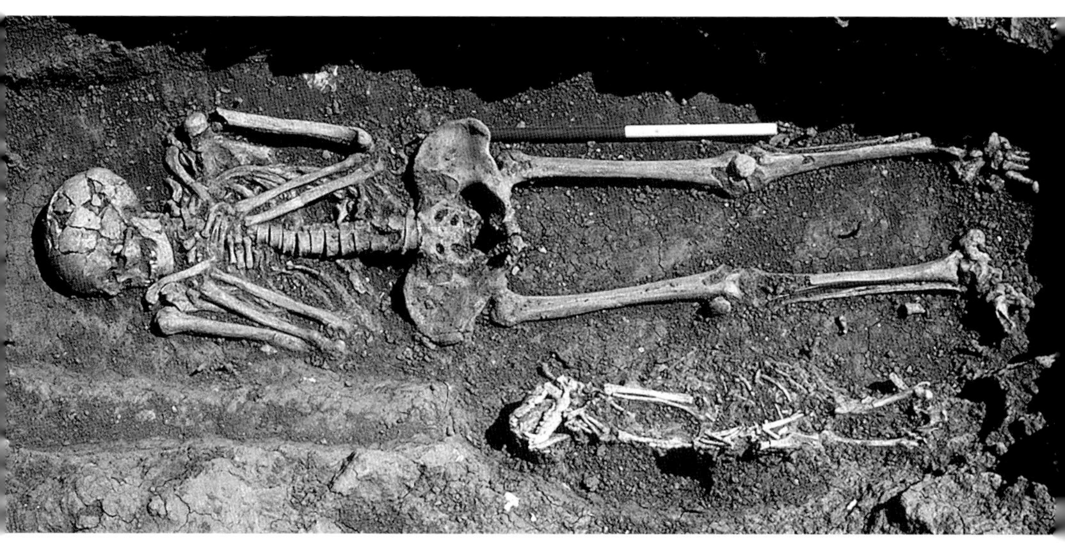

'One man and his dog' – burial of a man with a dog in the south-western suburbs beside the Fosse Way at Ilchester.

particular was high. Most of those buried in these cemeteries belonged to the lower orders of society, as were those in similar groups of burials found at Shepton Mallet, but some graves clearly represent wealthier and more influential members of the community.

Across the river from Ilchester, in the suburb of Northover, was a much larger cemetery, which was in use from the later third century and on into the fifth. It has been estimated that a minimum of 1500 people lie here, and probably several hundreds more. Of the handful investigated, most represent the ordinary citizens of Ilchester, but among them were occasional burials in lead and stone coffins. In a few instances a stone sarcophagus contained a coffin made of folded lead sheet, while in others the body was buried in only a lead coffin, or just a stone sarcophagus. The lead is likely to have come from the Mendip mines, while the stone was quarried on Ham Hill. The employment of such materials for burial implies that these individuals were from the wealthier families of Roman Ilchester, although objects buried with them have rarely been found. Almost all the graves located in the Northover cemetery were aligned broadly east-west, and occasional finds of coins or pottery in their backfill suggest that most of the graves date to the fourth century or later, when many people were abandoning the old pagan beliefs and adopting Christianity. The east-west grave orientations and lack of items placed with the burials could suggest that Ilchester had a large Christian community by this time, though there is no conclusive proof for this assumption.

In the countryside burials are sometimes found close to farms and

Child burial within a stone coffin at the Fosse Lane settlement, Shepton Mallet.

villas. Rural communities normally buried their dead in a designated spot on the property. One of the best examples was at the fourth-century farm at Bradley Hill, near Somerton, where 37 of the 55 excavated burials were infants. Many of the latter were buried beneath the floor of one of the buildings and could represent unwanted offspring disposed of by slave workers. The high number of infants also illustrates the harshness of life in rural Roman Somerset, as well as the vulnerability of the young and newborn to illness and adversity. Infant burials are relatively common in and around buildings, where some appear to have been buried in unorthodox ways, rather than formally in a cemetery. Sometimes infants were buried beneath doorways, within walls or below their foundations, suggesting a deliberate act of ritual significance. There are examples from buildings in Ilchester, Shepton Mallet and Camerton, as well as on other rural sites.

Once again, people of higher status are indicated by their coffins, usually of lead or stone, and occasionally by valuable objects placed near the body. Discoveries of stone coffins with burials at the villas of Combe Down and Newton St Loe near Bath probably represent members of the wealthy landowner's family. At Ilchester Mead a lead coffin containing a young girl was found buried immediately in front of the villa courtyard entrance, perhaps a greatly loved daughter of the owner's buried close to home. At Shepton Mallet, another young child was buried within a stone coffin found in one of the backplots behind buildings in the town there.

TEN

Somerset after the Romans

In AD 410 the then Roman emperor Honorius wrote to the *civitates* of Britain informing them that they should look to their own defence. Effectively the imperial government of the province had collapsed and it was now up to the individual local authorities to take responsibility for their own affairs.

How had this situation come about? Although the historical sources are sketchy for this period, we know that during the last decades of the fourth century the Roman Empire, particularly in the west, was under increasing pressure from outside its borders. Barbarian raiders like the Franks, Goths, Saxons, and even the Irish and the Picts from Scotland, were a serious threat to Britain and Western Europe; a situation compounded by internal rebellions in some provinces. In Britain, a series of military usurpers attempted coups to claim the imperial throne, with the support of army divisions still garrisoning the frontiers of the province. None of these attempts were ultimately successful, but must have further weakened the ties with Rome. By the early fifth century the citizens of Britain were being forced to take control of their own destinies. To make matters worse there were serious barbarian raids upon the province in 408, as a result of which the imperial government seems to have been overthrown and replaced.

The letter from Honorius in 410 may simply have been recognition of a de facto situation, but despite this seemingly firm end date, much of the character and fabric of late Roman Britain was maintained for another century or more. How then was Somerset affected by these processes, and what kind of evidence survives by which we might gain an insight into this transition between the ancient classical world and that which was to become our own?

TOWNS AND GOVERNMENT

Perhaps the greatest problem faced by archaeologists and historians of this period is the relative paucity of evidence. Reliable documentary sources are few and far between, while the interpretation of archaeological evidence is seriously hampered by the scarcity of well-dated material. Coinage, particularly in the fourth century, was for the most part common and widespread, allowing relatively precise structural dating. With the break from Rome this supply ceased – there was no longer an imperial army or civil service to pay. Britain's new insularity also impacted upon the established social and economic fabric of society. Long established patterns of trade broke down. The production and distribution of metalwork and pottery began to fail, and both exporting and importing virtually ceased. The wealth and security of many landowners was threatened, forcing them to abandon their country estates for the towns. Christianity now began to dominate society, affecting burial customs and religious observance, while building in stone and mortar declined and eventually appears to have died out. All of these factors, and others, create difficulties in both recognising and dating archaeological evidence relating to this immediately post-Roman period in Britain, and thus our understanding of what was happening in Somerset.

Both of Somerset's main towns – Bath and Ilchester – later became important medieval towns, and their sites are still occupied today. This has resulted in successive disturbance of their surviving Roman fabric, and especially of remains that belong to the final phases of occupation. Massive stone walls and gates enclosed their centres in the fourth century, features that persisted until medieval refurbishment (at Bath) or rebuilding (at Ilchester), several centuries later. These defences could at least guarantee some security and stability for the newly independent governments of Britain. At first these were presumably based closely upon their predecessors within the imperial system. In Somerset, Bath and Ilchester, at the centres of two of the wealthiest regions of late Roman Britain, are likely to have continued as political, administrative and military centres for their regions.

Perhaps we should imagine a system akin to the independent classical city-state, or the medieval Italian city-states, but what was life like within the walls of Bath or Ilchester? Glimpses provided by recent excavations in Bath suggest that some buildings were in a state of decay by the late fourth century, although re-building with timber appears to have persisted well into the fifth century, both within the walls and beyond in Walcot. At Abbeygate Street a sequence of Roman buildings ended with decay and collapse at the end of the fourth century, before being followed by another building sequence, which might have spanned much of the fifth century. The discovery of a severed head of a young woman within an abandoned oven tragically illustrates the insecurities and hazards of those times.

The baths and sacred spring complex in Bath seem to have been badly affected by periodic flooding of the River Avon during the fourth century; a process which eventually led to their being abandoned as they were overwhelmed by silting in the fifth century. Within the temple

Debris from the eventual collapse and demolition of the temple of Sulis Minerva, Bath.

precinct the paved surround was gradually buried beneath silt and by rubbish derived from occupation elsewhere in the town, although there were also attempts to maintain new floor levels. The popularity and patronage of the whole complex must have been under increasing threat through the fourth century, with the rise of Christianity. The inscription on an altar dedicated by Gaius Severius Emeritus suggests the restoration of a shrine 'wrecked by insolent hands' *(see chapter 4)*. By the fifth century it is unlikely that the pagan rituals centred upon the worship of Sulis Minerva would have been tolerated any longer. However, the temple building evidently survived more or less intact for several centuries, and it may be that the continued use and refurbishing of the precinct reflects a rededication of the temple as a Christian church. It is perhaps significant that the Anglo-Saxon monastic community founded by Osric in 675 AD was located immediately to the east of the temple, perhaps then finally replacing it and re-using its stone.

At Ilchester the scale of excavation, particularly within the walls, has been too small, and the degree of medieval and later disturbances too great, to gain any clear evidence for buildings or occupation lasting long into the fifth century. Town life appears to have flourished right to the end of the fourth century, when reliable dates cease, and could well have been maintained for much longer behind the security of its walls. In the suburbs, the intensity of occupation evidently declined in the last decades of the fourth century, although there are traces of later timber-framed structures above derelict stone buildings, and burial in the plots behind the road-frontage buildings probably increased as their occupation declined. In the Northover cemetery there are instances of burials cut into graves containing late fourth-century (Theodosian) coins, suggesting that burial there was still continuing. This cemetery, with the possibility of late Roman Christian burials, lies adjacent to the later Saxon minster church of St Andrew in the (once) separate parish of Northover; another hint perhaps of post-Roman continuity in a Christian context.

The small roadside town at Shepton Mallet lay almost entirely beyond the bounds of any medieval or later settlement. This good fortune has provided archaeologists with an opportunity to look for remains of the last phase of Roman settlement over extensive areas, in advance of modern development. Once again there is evidence for timber-framed buildings replacing stone buildings of the fourth century, and sometimes the recycling of materials such as stone roof tiles (to line graves and post-holes), or door and window jambs (in steps or paving). Dating for these events or their duration beyond the end of the fourth century is hard to come by. With the assistance of radio-carbon dates (C14) some of the burials provide a better idea of the time scale involved.

Over fifty burials have been excavated among the remains of the Fosse Lane settlement, the majority placed within and apparently respecting pre-existing boundaries or enclosures, although a few were cut into the remains of earlier structures. Only a small number have been sampled for radio-carbon dating, and all seem to be of late or post-Roman date. One group of east-west burials included a woman in a lead coffin, and a mature man buried with a unique silver pendant decorated with a monogrammed cross. This appears to be one of the few instances of a demonstrable Christian burial in late Roman Britain (possibly around AD 400). The present Archbishop of Canterbury (Bishop of Bath and Wells at the time of its discovery) wears a silver replica of the cross – a gift from the then owners of the site, Showerings Ltd. This burial and another in the group have radio-carbon determinations that indicate a late fourth or fifth century date, and suggest that a small Christian community was then living here.

Some of the graves at Shepton Mallet were not aligned east-west and included features such as decapitation, and the inclusion of coins, animal remains, hobnailed boots or pottery vessels, which normally

A silver pendant decorated with a monogrammed cross from an early Christian burial at Shepton Mallet.

signify pagan burial rites. Interestingly, two of these graves had radiocarbon dates that should place them in the fifth or even the sixth century, which would suggest that pagans may have co-existed alongside Christians in some post-Roman communities. One of these burials was within a rather crude lead coffin, and nearby a stone coffin made of re-used building stone was surrounded by the foundations of what appears to be a mausoleum. Such features, along with other lead and stone coffins from the town, suggest the continuation of a degree of wealth and social stratification within this late and post-Roman society.

However long occupation may have continued at places like Shepton Mallet, Ilchester or Bath, these were no longer truly urban societies. Trade and industry was drastically reduced, public services and the maintenance of streets, water supplies or stone buildings virtually ceased. Animals were kept and even crops grown within the towns as the

A late Roman burial within a stone coffin made of re-used architectural fragments and surrounded by the foundations of a mausoleum, at Fosse Lane, Shepton Mallet.

population declined: rubbish accumulated everywhere. With the social, political and economic disruption of the early fifth century and the final break with Rome, there was no longer a system within which an urban society could flourish. Those with strong defensive walls like Bath and Ilchester now became the power bases for the new governing elite, almost certainly dominated by individual leaders. This was in some respects a return to the old tribal confederations that the Romans found or created at the time of their conquest, but now within a very different world. The emergence of these new leaders and their territories, based perhaps upon the old *civitates*, in Britain as well as in Western Europe, heralds the British, Anglo-Saxon and eventually the medieval kingdoms that were to follow.

THE COUNTRYSIDE

By the fourth century Roman Britain may have had a population of over five million, the great majority of whom lived and worked in the countryside. As the century advanced Somerset's prosperity was threatened by a variety of factors, including ever increasing taxation and inflation, labour shortages, revolts of local slaves and peasants disaffected by growing hardships, the progressive weakening of effective central government, and perhaps above all by the external threat from barbarian peoples on the frontiers of the empire.

Factors such as these were already prompting the building of walls around towns of all sizes from the end of the third century, but in the countryside farms, villages, temples and the wealthy villa estates were more vulnerable. Almost without exception, evidence from excavation of these sites in Somerset show a marked decline in their status or even their abandonment during the last decades of the century. This is a pattern repeated throughout Britain at this time, although once again, the lack of material datable to the fifth century or later makes it hard to assess the duration or true scope of these changes.

One particularly severe attack on Britain was recorded in AD 367, when a supposed conspiracy involving Picts, Irish and Saxon raiders plundered large parts of the province. This undoubtedly alarmed the Romano-British, who seem until then to have been relatively free of such troubles (more prevalent in Continental Europe); due in part to being protected by the sea and a system of coastal forts, as well as the northern garrison on Hadrian's Wall. The effect of this incursion and the increasing insecurity felt by the whole population probably had a major impact upon the relative affluence of late Roman Britain.

Where excavations on a sufficient scale have taken place, it appears that most villa buildings either suffered a marked decline in standards of maintenance and the quality of their occupation, or in some instances

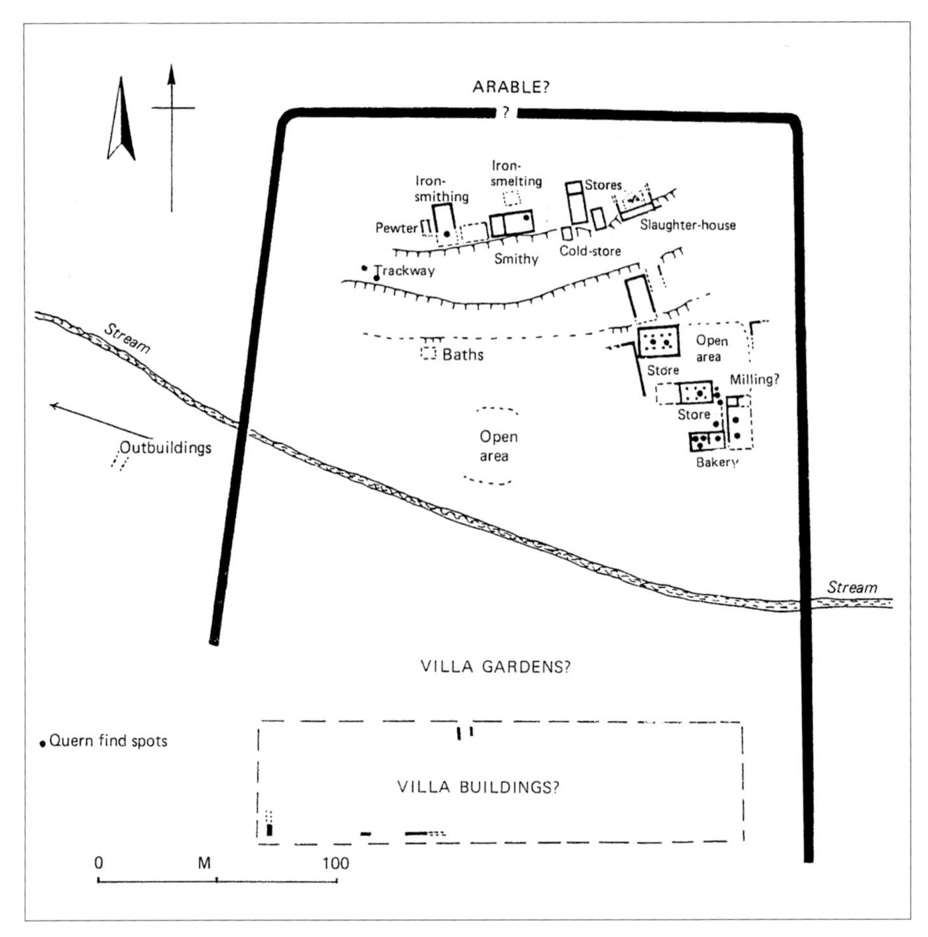

Plan of the settlement at Gatcombe, a villa estate fortified by a wall in the fourth century, with an interpretation of the function of excavated buildings and areas.

were even abandoned during the last decades of the fourth century. Abandonment is suspected at Westland and at Lufton near Yeovil, at Wemberham and at Chew Park, while other villas like Keynsham, Combe Down or Wellow near Bath were affected by major fires around this time. Such evidence is not necessarily attributable to a specific episode of disruption such as the 367 raids, but may be symptomatic of changes in the status and fortunes of these estates. In fact, there is frequently evidence for activity and occupation that seems to have continued to the end of the fourth century and beyond.

At Ilchester Mead a new building was erected within the main courtyard and partly over the demolished corridor of the main house. New stone floors and occupation debris sealed mosaic pavements at Lufton, and there are remains of late structures replacing or impinging upon the main buildings at Low Ham and West Coker. Many villas betray evidence of a change of use for the main buildings in their final phase of occupation, including the insertion of ovens or corn-drying kilns in former living rooms, as at Keynsham, Ilchester Mead or Newton St Loe.

At Gatcombe, the villa and its adjacent buildings were surrounded by a defensive boundary wall, a feature recorded quite frequently on the Continent (but so far unique in Roman Britain), where instability and disruption had been much more widespread in the countryside since the third century. Unfortunately, the building of the railway largely destroyed the Gatcombe villa in the nineteenth century, and thus we know nothing of its history, although the ancillary buildings were still in use until at least the end of the fourth century.

Virtually all the evidence from Somerset's villas, and from elsewhere in Britain, indicates a change in their use and status during the last years of the fourth century. As in the towns, a virtual absence of datable finds makes it difficult to estimate the duration of the final phases of occupation. What appears to have happened was a move back into the better protected towns by the villa owners and their families (where many already had houses), leaving their estates to be managed and worked by bailiffs, servants and slaves. The now deserted villa buildings could then be used for more mundane agricultural activities, and for residence by the estate workers. Even in times of crisis and upheaval, the agricultural estates will have survived and farming continued, providing that there was the manpower and the continuity of ownership. This may have become increasingly tenuous as the fifth century progressed, but the ownership and control of land and its resources was still the principal basis for power and prestige in late and post-Roman Britain.

The later history of the majority of humbler rural settlements in Somerset is less clear. At the village of Catsgore it has been suggested that occupation ceased from around AD 370, although life and death (burials) continued on the nearby farm at Bradley Hill to the end of the fourth century and beyond. No other such settlements in Somerset have been excavated on a sufficiently extensive scale to adequately determine the full character or duration of their occupation. Evidence from sites like Sigwells or Podimore in the south, Holway or Maidenbrook Farm near Taunton, or Butcombe near Bristol Airport, suggest that they flourished through much of the fourth century. There are clear signs of retraction on the Levels, north and south of Mendip, but this can in part be attributed to rising sea levels, as well as a breakdown in the maintenance of river and sea flood defences. Once again, the lack of good dating material means that we have little evidence for the final chapters in the history of the county's smaller settlements, although much of the land continued to be worked and people to live on it, despite their virtual invisibility after the early fifth century.

The impact of Christianity has already been seen in Somerset's three principal towns, but its presence was also felt in the countryside. By its nature, Christianity leaves little archaeological trace at this early period; there are no indisputable fourth or fifth-century churches yet recognised in Somerset, and even burials can rarely identify a Christian community with any certainty. Since the time of the emperor Constantine the Great, early in the fourth century, Christianity had been the official religion of the Empire, and may thus have been adopted first in the towns. In the troubled late fourth century it might well have appealed particularly to the more disadvantaged members of society, many of whom lived in the countryside.

From another perspective the vigour and popularity of pagan beliefs throughout much of the fourth century is especially evident at the rural temple sites, due to their patronage by the essentially conservative and still largely pagan, land-owning aristocracy. The architectural development, and sometimes foundation, of these temples certainly equates with the era of maximum prosperity for the villas of Somerset. By the end of the fourth century most of the great landowners had probably adopted Christianity, a move coinciding with the gradual decline and abandonment of most temples and other places of pagan worship.

Despite this great religious reorientation of society some pagan temple sites may have been Christianised. At the two very similar hilltop shrines on Lamyatt Beacon and Brean Down, small, single-cell stone buildings, aligned east-west, were placed in almost identical positions close to the earlier temples. A small cemetery of east-west graves with radio-carbon dates in the sixth and seventh centuries lay just to the north of the Lamyatt building. At Brean Down, another cemetery with comparable radio-carbon dates lies a little further away in the sand cliff to the east. At Henley Wood a similarly dated cemetery of up to 90 burials, aligned broadly east-west, lay mainly to the east of the temple remains, with a few graves cut into it. There was no evidence of a later building alongside, although the north and west temple exteriors had already been destroyed by quarrying before the site could be excavated. No later buildings or post-Roman burials were found at Pagans Hill, but the discovery of an iron pail and a decorated glass jar within the well, both of seventh-century Anglo-Saxon origin, suggests some continuing use, and perhaps veneration of the site.

There are several other suspected post-Roman burial sites in Somerset, e.g. Portishead, Wint Hill Villa, Banwell, or Wembdon, Bridgwater, but the largest and most thoroughly explored was at

A seventh-century Anglo-Saxon glass jar from the temple well at Pagans Hill.

Cannington, on a limestone hilltop overlooking the estuary of the River Parrett. Over 500 excavated burials survived from a cemetery which probably contained at least three times that number originally, radiocarbon dates suggesting interments over a period from at least the fourth century until the seventh or eighth. Most were aligned broadly east-west, and an early focus for the cemetery may have been a small circular shrine near the top of the hill containing the grave of a young man. A later focus for burial was the probable seventh-century grave of a young woman in a stone cist marked by an engraved slab and approached from the north by a path. There are no clear pagan associations with this site and it may have been a Christian burial ground founded in the late Roman period, possibly containing graves of local saints or holy men, which continued in use until or after the Anglo-Saxon take-over of Somerset. Early Christian memorial stones commemorating individuals, a notable survival of this period in parts of western Britain, are also found occasionally in West Somerset, perhaps the most important being the Caratacus stone on Winford Hill *(see overleaf for illustration)*. Such memorials are surely indicators of a literate Christian elite within fifth and sixth century society.

An early Christian memorial stone, the 'Caratacus stone' on Winford Hill, Exmoor.

THE END OF ROMAN SOMERSET

Two battles recorded in the 'Anglo-Saxon Chronicle' seem to mark the ultimate end of Roman Somerset. In AD 577 the Battle of Dyrham records the capture of Bath (still perhaps a significant and occupied place within its walls?), and in AD 658 a battle at Penselwood, on the Somerset/Wiltshire border, probably brought all but the western extremities of the county into the kingdom of Wessex. However, in the period between the official end of Roman rule and the arrival of the Anglo-Saxons there were radical changes in the whole fabric of society in the county. A clear understanding of this period is hampered by a dearth of both historical and archaeological evidence, but in Somerset we have good glimpses of the settlements, religion and burial, and social organisation of a time which is as enigmatic as any in the county's past.

Somerset spans something of a cultural and geographical divide. Broadly speaking, this divide was expressed politically in both the Iron Age and Roman periods, and seems to have persisted into the post-Roman period. By the end of the fifth century a new system had evolved out of the ashes of the Romano-British provinces, which may have divided Somerset politically, much as it had done for the past half millennium and more. To the west, beyond the River Parrett, was the kingdom of Dumnonia, based on the earlier tribal and *civitas* lands of the Dumnonii. Its political centre may initially have been the old Roman *civitas* capital at Exeter, but from the late fifth century this was transferred to the defended promontory of Tintagel, on the north coast of Cornwall.

As has already been suggested, the late Roman *civitas* capital of the northern Durotriges at Ilchester was the natural base for a new and independent regional government, but once again there seems to have been a move late in the fifth century to a new fortified centre. This was to the old Iron Age hillfort at Cadbury Castle, which was heavily re-fortified and then re-occupied for the best part of a century. This was perhaps a power base for a new Durotrigan kingdom or state, although its relationship with Dorchester and the Dorset Durotriges is not clear. The old Dobunnic region of north Somerset may have come under the administration of a state or kingdom based at Bath, although it has been suggested that it was more probably part of a larger state centred on the original Dobunnic *civitas* capital at Cirencester, which had become the capital of the late Roman province of *Britannia Prima*. What may have marked the frontier between these states is a bank and ditch earthwork known as the Wansdyke, which in Somerset extends from Dundry Hill near Bristol to cross the Avon into Wiltshire east of Bath. If correct, this suggests that the old boundary between the Durotriges and the Dobunni

The south west gate, Cadbury Castle, re-fortified in the sixth century.

had moved northwards and that Bath was now close to its frontier. Alternatively the Wansdyke may have been built to separate the south-eastern British kingdoms from the Anglo Saxons, following the Battle of Dyrham.

We do not have the names of these new states or kingdoms, although like Dumnonia, they were probably close to those of their Roman predecessors. Unlike Dumnonia, they did not last as long, and were eventually overrun by their Anglo-Saxon neighbours. In their heyday these western British states were the direct heirs of the Romano-British citizens and governments of Somerset and the West Country. Once established they were probably relatively prosperous, and perhaps not seriously threatened by either their Saxon neighbours to the east, or the Irish and Picts to the north and west. At times they may have quarrelled with each other, although they were capable of forging alliances against a common threat, as the legend of King Arthur and the victory against the Saxons at Mount Badon seems to suggest

From the late fifth and the earlier sixth century direct links were once more established with the Roman world, for a time on the ascendant again in the guise of the Byzantine Empire as the heirs to Rome. This contact led to the importing of distinctive east-Mediterranean and North African pottery, as well as occasional glass and metalwork. Some of this reached Somerset, and helps to identify and date some settlement

Glastonbury Tor – an early Christian monastic site from the fifth and sixth centuries.

and burial sites of the period.

One of the largest collections has come from another re-fortified Iron Age hillfort, at Cadbury Congresbury, where several circular and rectangular timber buildings were located within the defences. The site lies adjacent to the seemingly contemporary cemetery beside the earlier pagan temple at Henley Wood, which is likely to have been the burial place of many of its inhabitants. Similar pottery has come from Cadbury Castle, although no cemetery has yet been found there. Several other hillforts around Somerset may have been re-occupied at this time, perhaps as the strongholds of local leaders. The Cannington cemetery also has a little of this Mediterranean pottery, and lies adjacent to another hillfort with potential for re-occupation.

Pottery from the Mediterranean has also been found at two sites which may have been early Christian monasteries; Carhampton near Dunster, where there were also burials and evidence for metalworking, and on the summit of Glastonbury Tor. On this very exposed hilltop were traces of buildings and more evidence for metalworking, but no burials. Was this perhaps the kernel of Glastonbury's great medieval monastic heritage? Similarly, the contemporary burials and the small chapel or oratory-like buildings adjacent to the earlier temples on Brean Down and Lamyatt Beacon could identify these sites as further early Christian monasteries, appropriately sited on relatively remote hilltops.

The fifth and sixth centuries, sometimes referred to as the Dark Ages, mark a watershed in our history. They represent a time of evolution from the prehistoric and ancient worlds, of which Britain and Europe had been a part, to the new world of medieval Europe. This was, perhaps, an inevitable process, but fascinating new evidence for a major worldwide natural catastrophe at this time may have given it new impetus. What seems to have been either a large cometary impact or a major volcanic eruption has been recognised, mainly through dendrochronolgy (study of tree growth rings) and ice-core sampling, to have occurred around AD 540. This could be linked with other roughly contemporary recorded events around the world; notably the disastrous plague which affected all Europe, including Britain, in the following decade. These are controversial theories, but were perhaps a final prelude to the expansion of the Anglo-Saxon kingdom of Wessex, and the emergence for the first time of the County of Somerset.

Places to Visit

BATH, ROMAN BATHS MUSEUM. The most impressive displays of both finds and remains still in situ in Somerset. Remains include the sacred spring, the Great Bath, and other parts of the baths and temple precinct, and a fine display of sculpture, inscriptions and other finds from the baths and temple complex, as well as from other sites in and around Bath, including Camerton.

BREAN DOWN, near Weston-super-Mare. Iron Age hillfort, prehistoric/Romano-British field systems. The temple site is not visible.

BRENT KNOLL, near Burnham-on Sea. Iron Age hillfort, possible late Roman temple site, views over the Somerset Levels.

BRIDGWATER, ADMIRAL BLAKE MUSEUM. Roman material from local sites, including Combwich and Crandon Bridge.

BRISTOL CITY MUSEUM. Roman material from North Somerset sites, including Gatcombe, Keynsham villa (mosaics) and Pagans Hill.

BRYMPTON D'EVERCY HOUSE, YEOVIL. Mosaic pavement from Westland villa.

CADBURY CASTLE, SOUTH CADBURY. Iron Age hillfort, possible temple site, post-Roman re-fortification, and extensive views over South Somerset.

CADBURY CONGRESBURY. Iron Age hillfort, post-Roman re-fortification, Henley Wood temple site (no visible remains).

CHARTERHOUSE ON MENDIP. Lead mining settlement earthworks, amphitheatre remains, Roman fort remains, lead mining rakes.

DOLEBURY, CHURCHILL. Iron Age hillfort, well preserved defences, internal settlement features.

FOSSE WAY. Much of this road in Somerset is now replaced by modern highways but a good stretch survives as a green lane between Beacon Hill and

Shepton Mallet, and as the A37 for most of the route between Shepton Mallet and Ilchester.

GLASTONBURY. TOR – early Christian monastery (no visible remains), TRIBUNAL MUSEUM, High Street – Iron Age lake village finds and reconstruction model.

HAM HILL, STOKE-SUB-HAMDON. Country Park. Very large Iron Age hillfort, stone quarries, villa site (no visible remains), proposed information centre.

ILCHESTER. Roman town site (no visible remains), MUSEUM – small display of Roman and later remains from the town.

SHEPTON MALLET. TOURIST INFORMATION CENTRE – small display of finds from the Roman town site, TESCO STORES, FOSSE LANE – information board on excavations and discoveries in cafeteria.

SOMERSET COUNTY MUSEUM, TAUNTON CASTLE. Displays of material from Somerset sites including, Ilchester, Catsgore, Lamyatt Beacon, Brean Down, Shepton Mallet, Shapwick, South Cadbury and villas, including the Low Ham 'Dido and Aeneas' pavement.

WATCHET, MARKET HOUSE MUSEUM. Material from local Romano-British sites.

WELLS MUSEUM. Material from local Romano-British sites, including Wookey Hole, Charterhouse, and other Mendip lead mining sites.

WESTON-SUPER-MARE MUSEUM. Displays and finds from local sites including Locking and Wemberham villas, and from Congresbury and Henley Wood.

WORLBURY, WESTON-SUPER-MARE. Iron Age hillfort, well preserved defences, possible temple site.

YEOVIL, MUSEUM OF SOUTH SOMERSET. Displays and finds from local villas and other sites including, Westland, Lufton, Ilchester Mead and Cadbury Castle.

Further Reading

Good general accounts of the history and character of Roman Britain include *The Oxford Illustrated History of Roman Britain*, Peter Salway, Oxford 1993; *Britannia, A History of Roman Britain*, S.S. Frere, London 1987; and *The Romanization of Britain*, Martin Millett, Cambridge 1990.

Other books provide a good background on more specific topics, including *Iron Age Communities in Britain*, B.W. Cunliffe, London 1991; *The Small Towns of Roman Britain*, B. Burnham and J. Wacher, Batsford 1990; *The Landscape of Roman Britain*, K. Dark and P. Dark, Sutton 1997; *Britain and the End of the Roman Empire*, K. Dark, Tempus 2000; *The Golden Age of Roman Britain*, G. de la Bedoyere, Tempus 1999, *The Buildings of Roman Britain*, G. de la Bedoyere, Tempus 2001; *The Ending of Roman Britain*, S. Esmonde Cleary, Batsford 1989; *Religion in Roman Britain*, M. Henig, Batsford 1984; *Rural Settlement in Roman Britain*, R. Hingley, Seaby 1989.

This is the first book devoted to Roman Somerset, although the earliest account was by F.J. Haverfield in Volume I of the *Victoria County History of Somerset*, 1906, which although now long out of date, is probably still the most wide ranging survey of Roman sites and remains in the county. More recent overviews have appeared in broader-based surveys of Somerset, beginning with *The Archaeology of Somerset*, D. Dobson, 1931; *The Archaeology of Somerset*, edited by M. Aston and I. Burrow, Somerset County Council 1982, and most recently *The Origins of Somerset*, Michael Costen, Manchester 1992.

Several specific aspects of the period in Somerset were usefully reviewed in *The Roman West Country*, edited by K. Brannigan and P. Fowler, David and Charles 1976, although now somewhat out of date. Another valuable review is 'The Roman Interlude in the South West: the Dynamics of Social and Economic Change in Romano-British South Somerset and North Dorset' by Roger Leech and published in *The Romano-British Countryside: Studies in Rural Settlement and Economy*, edited by David Miles, BAR no.103, Oxford 1982. A more recent overview of the central and north Somerset Levels appears in *The Severn Estuary, Landscape Evolution and Wetland Reclamation*, Stephen Rippon, Leicester 1997.

The prime source for information on many of the Roman sites and discoveries within the county is the annual *Proceedings of the Somerset Archaeological and Natural History Society*, who are based at the Castle in Taunton. Another periodical source is the *Proceedings of the University of Bristol Spelaeological Society*, which covers some of the Mendip and north Somerset sites. Basic data on all recorded sites in the county is held by the three local authorities who now administer the historic county of Somerset and maintain computerised Sites and Monuments Records. These are based at County Hall, Taunton for Somerset, Somerset House, Weston-super-Mare for North Somerset and at Trimbridge House, Bath for Bath and North East Somerset.

The detailed publication of material and evidence for many of the sites featured in this account has now been achieved, particularly in recent years. Several monograph volumes have published the results of excavations and research in Bath over the last few decades, as well as papers in other academic journals. However, by far the most accessible account of Roman Bath and its archaeology is *Roman Bath Discovered*, by Barry Cunliffe, Tempus 2000, which also lists many of the other academic publications. The only popular publication for Ilchester is a booklet produced in 1990 by the County Council – *Ilchester*, by Peter Leach and Robert Dunning, though now out of print. Two detailed volumes of published archaeological research, however, are *Ilchester Volume 1. Excavations 1974-75*, P. Leach, Bristol 1982, and *Ilchester Volume 2. Archaeology, Excavations and Fieldwork to 1984*, P. Leach, Sheffield 1994; as well as other shorter works published by the Somerset Archaeological and Natural History Society. Another popular publication also out of print, for Shepton Mallet, is *Shepton Mallet, Romano-Britons and Early Christians in Somerset*, P. Leach, Birmingham 1991, although once again, a volume is now published detailing the discoveries made there in 1990, *Fosse Lane: Excavations of a Romano-British Roadside Settlement at Shepton Mallet, Somerset*, P. Leach with J. Evans, The Roman Society Britannia Monograph No. 18, London 2001, and other publications are forthcoming.

Other sites in Somerset published individually as monograph volumes are Camerton - *Excavations at Camerton, Somerset*, W. Wedlake, Bath 1958; Chew – *Excavations at Chew Valley Lake, Somerset*, P. Rahtz and E. Greenfield, H.M.SO. 1977; Gatcombe – *Gatcombe Roman Villa*, K. Brannigan, BAR 44, Oxford 1977; Catsgore – *Excavations at Catsgore 1970-1973. A Romano-British Village*, R. Leech, Bristol 1982; Cadbury Congresbury – *Cadbury Congresbury 1968-1973: a late/post-Roman hilltop settlement in Somerset,* P. Rahtz et al., BAR, Oxford 1992; Henley Wood – *Henley Wood, Temples and Cemetery Excavations 1962-69,* L. Watts and P. Leach, CBA Research Report 99, York 1996; Cannington – *Cannington Cemetery*, P. Rahtz, S. Wright & S. Hirst, The Roman Society Britannia Monograph No. 17, London 2000; and Cadbury Castle – *Cadbury Castle, Somerset*, J. Barrett, P. Freeman and A. Woodward, English Heritage Archaeological Report 20, London 2000.

By no means all of the publications cited are now in print, but the most comprehensive collection of books, articles and journals relating to Roman archaeology in Somerset is to be found in the Somerset Studies Library, Taunton Public Library, Paul Street, Taunton.

Index